Contents

Acknowledgements

We would like to thank all the housing associations and local authorities who co-operated with this research, the National Federation of Housing Associations and the Housing Corporation.

In addition, we wish to thank those housing applicants who gave up their time to be interviewed as part of this study.

This research was carried out for the Department of the Environment by the Centre for Housing Management and Development at the University of Wales College of Cardiff.

Department of the Environment

Access, Allocations and Nominations: The Role of Housing Associations

John Parker
Robert Smith
Peter Williams

London: HMSO

First published 1992
Second impression 1994

ISBN 0 11 752725 4

List of tables

NOTE

In the tables listed above the basic figure for individual tabulations of new applicants and new lettings may vary. This is explained by missing individual values for particular variables.

Additionally, percentage figures in individual tables have been rounded up or down to the nearest whole number. As a result columns do not always add to 100%.

[illegible]

[illegible]

[illegible]

Summary

Purpose of research

This study was undertaken during the period July 1990 to August 1991. Its purpose was as follows:-

(a) To examine housing association allocation policies and current practices.

(b) To assess the relationship between local authorities and house associations in terms of needs assessment and nomination arrangements.

Key findings

The study was conducted by means of 6 local case studies. Each one comprised several components, namely; interviews with the local authority and a sample of the larger housing associations; analysis of information related to new applicants and recent lettings; group and in-depth interviews with a small number of recent applicants (see para 1.21).

- The research has shown that associations are providing a diverse range of general family and special needs accommodation (see chapter 2).
- The surveys of associations and consumers suggest that there is a lack of information about the general role of associations. This has an impact on who applies to associations (see paras 2.13 to 2.23).
- Outside of London the majority of associations maintained open waiting lists whilst in the capital, lists were often closed and associations relied largely upon nominations and referrals (see paras 2.24 to 2.38).
- The largest group of new applicants to associations were single adults, particularly the younger age groups. Households with children were the second largest group (see paras 2.39 to 2.67).
- Analysis of new lettings confirmed that associations were meeting their primary objective of housing people in need. However their ability to meet the range of needs is limited by the profile of their housing stock which tends to be dominated by one and two bedroom properties (see paras 3.9 - 3.19).
- The pattern of allocations shows that single adults under pensionable age accounted for the largest proportion of lettings. The elderly were the second most significant group (see paras 3.20 - 3.21).
- Nominations were not an insignificant component of the local authorities' direct housing role. However in relation to total lettings by the authorities themselves, nominations were small in number (see paras 4.3 to 4.9).
- Elderly people were one third of successful nominees whilst families accounted for about two fifths. Over a third of all nominees were statutory homeless although this figure masked wide variation between London and elsewhere (see paras 4.18 to 4.34).

- The nominations process was found to be complex and inefficient. Neither local authorities nor associations were satisfied with the 'pool system' (see Glossary) as a method of organising nominations (see paras 4.35 to 4.45).
- There were evident gaps in the mechanisms needed to strategically plan the meeting of local housing needs. Local liaison arrangements were normally in place but these failed to ensure comprehensive planning to meet local needs (see paras 5.2 to 5.12).
- Consumer views of the application process were generally favourable. However, they revealed concerns about the lack of information on the application process, delays in communication and the absence of guidance on the allocation system (see paras 6.31 to 6.38).

Key recommendations

The findings of the study suggest a number of recommendations. These are as follows:

- The provision of better information about associations in general, and the application, allocation and nomination processes in particular.
- More regular contact with applicants regarding their applications and frequent updating of the information held on applicants.
- Associations should adopt more objective points-based systems for allocating their properties, which can be understood by applicants.
- Local authorities should adopt direct systems (see Glossary) for nominations (with nominees in priority order) rather than the pool based system.
- Performance targets should be set for nominations to improve the efficiency and effectiveness of the service offered to applicants, with in-built monitoring and review.
- Agreed mechanisms should be established for developing local housing strategies.
- Careful consideration should be given to how local authorities and housing associations might work together more closely in seeking to achieve their shared objective of meeting housing need.

Chapter 1 Introduction

Background to the research

1.1 The importance of housing associations as providers of social housing is growing rapidly and their role is changing, especially in relation to rehousing homeless people. It is for these two main reasons that the Department of the Environment (DoE) commissioned the research into housing association allocations policies reported here.

1.2 Until recently housing associations have been seen as providing a supporting and complementary role to the main providers of affordable rented housing - the local authorities. Now it is the associations that are regarded by Government as the main providers of new and rehabilitated dwellings, and moreover, they are being encouraged to extend their activities by taking over the management of the existing local authority housing stock.

1.3 With such changes taking place it is evident that the established allocation policies and practices of housing associations may no longer be appropriate. It is appropriate therefore to examine current practices, to test how well they are working and to see what changes may be required to meet the new circumstances and challenges.

1.4 In relation to allocations there are two fundamental issues which need to be considered;

a) access to the stock e.g. how potential applicants get to know about and apply to associations, the systems that are used to select tenants once they have applied and the effectiveness and fairness of these; and

b) the relationship between the local authority and housing associations in terms of the effectiveness of nomination arrangements and the question of how needs are assessed and translated into appropriate development programmes.

1.5 This study considers these issues by describing how the policies, procedures and practices of the agencies involved operate now and makes an assessment of their effectiveness in terms of current and future needs.

The role of housing associations in the '70s and early '80s

1.6 Although the voluntary housing movement has a long history in the United Kingdom (e.g. the work of the Peabody and Guinness Trusts at the end of the last century) their contribution was relatively small until the expansion which followed the Housing Act of 1974. This Act expanded the role of the Housing Corporation (see Glossary) with the aim of promoting an increase of housing association activity. During this time associations were seen as providing a complementary role to the local authorities who remained the main providers of subsidised rented housing. The presumption was that associations would provide for those needs that were given a lower priority by local authorities such as single people, older people, those with special needs and people who needed to move from different areas of the country, especially for employment reasons.

1.7 Associations were also expected to assist local authorities by accepting nominations from them. The proportion of nominations to be provided was established as 50 per cent and this figure has become generally accepted, although a higher figure is sometimes used; for example, if the local authority contributes land towards a scheme.

Recent changes and their consequences

1.8 For a number of years it has been the stated aim of Government to change the role of local authorities from being primarily the main providers and managers of social housing to a new primary function as enablers. The first steps in this direction were implemented by changing the balance of housing public expenditure towards the Housing Corporation rather than local authorities. This was reinforced by the Housing Act 1988 and the Local Government and Housing Act 1989. As can be seen from Table 1.1 housing associations have gradually contributed a larger proportion of the total housing association and local authority new completions since 1981; rising from just over a quarter to just under a half in 1990. Under current policies it is likely that this proportion will continue to rise. This will feed into the lettings available to applicants which in 1989/90 were 230,000 in the local authority stock and 60,000 in association property.

1.9 The consequence of these changes is that something different is now being expected from housing associations. The policy implications of this for allocations were set out in Housing Corporation Circular HC/48/89 which called for a more rigorous approach to tenant selection and reminded associations of their statutory duty to assist local authorities in rehousing homeless people. However, many of the possible implications of the changed circumstances in which associations operate have yet to be examined in any great detail and a number of these are the subject of this report.

Table 1.1 **Permanent new dwellings completed by local authorities and housing associations, England 1981 - 1990**

Year	LAs	HAs	Total	HAs as % of Total
1981	46,000	16,800	62,800	27
1982	28,500	11,200	39,700	28
1983	28,500	14,300	42,800	33
1984	27,200	13,900	41,100	34
1985	22,500	11,400	33,900	34
1986	18,800	10,500	29,300	36
1987	15,700	10,600	26,300	40
1988	15,700	10,100	25,800	39
1989	13,900	9,600	23,500	41
1990	13,700	13,000	26,700	49

Source: DoE Housing and Construction Statistics.

1.10 In considering the implications of change it has to be recognised that housing associations are very diverse organisations. They range in size from national organisations with tens of thousands of dwellings, to very small organisations with just one or two, and they may work on a national, regional or very local scale. Although the voluntary service ethic is a strong and unifying force, associations have varied aims and objectives and management styles. Some look to provide for a complete range of housing needs while others specialise in particular aspects of need. Many run hostels and shared accommodation as well as managing self contained housing. Such diverse organisations need to (and will) react in different ways and at different speeds to the new challenges they have been presented with.

1.11 Within this varied spectrum a significant degree of uniformity and quality control is, of course, imposed by the Housing Corporation which is responsible for funding housing associations and controlling and monitoring their activities.

1.12 Diversity and flexibility have been seen by many as two of the main arguments for encouraging housing associations. They have catered for a wide range of needs, including some, such as housing for ex-offenders or ex-drug abusers, which many other housing agencies have preferred not to become involved with and they have been able to produce rapid solutions.

The research project

1.13 It is in the light of this background that the research project reported here has been carried out. The project has built upon existing research by the DoE (DoE 1991) and the National Federation of Housing Associations whose CORE system continuously monitors the kind of people who are housed by associations.

1.14 Compared to the information about who is housed, much less is known about how associations allocate their housing. It is clear from existing research that the associations do broadly cater for people in housing need but important issues are being raised about the effectiveness and fairness of the methods they use in choosing between groups and individuals in need. This is the subject of analysis in chapters 2 and 3 of the report.

1.15 Over the past few years the growth in homelessness and waiting lists has put increased pressure on local authorities while at the same time their housing stock has been declining through both right-to-buy sales and a sharp reduction in their new build programmes. These pressures have caused local authorities to take a greater interest in their nomination arrangements with associations which, until recently, many authorities have tended to operate in a very informal way. The nomination process is examined in chapter 4.

1.16 As local authorities take on an enabling role (see Glossary) and housing associations become more important as direct providers of housing, attention must also focus on the liaison arrangements which exist between the local authorities, the associations and the Housing Corporation. Building programmes and lettings policies must reflect the needs of the area and these needs not only have to be assessed but they must also be fed into the decision making processes of a large number of housing associations. In turn the consequences of programmes and policies must also be monitored and their effect on need reassessed. These issues are examined in chapter 5.

1.17 As housing associations grow in importance, it is becoming evident that more attention must be focused on providing a service geared to the needs of the targeted applicant groups and this includes the provision of information and advice and improving service delivery. These issues are taken up in chapter 6.

1.18 Finally in chapter 7 the issues are brought together, conclusions drawn and recommendations made.

Research methods used

1.19 A full account of the methodology used is set out in appendix B of this report.

1.20 The research adopted a case study approach. Six local authority areas with a significant number of housing association properties were selected (viz Bolton, Bromley, Camden, Derby, Exeter, and Leeds) with the aim of providing a wide regional spread (including an inner and an outer London borough), and a range of different housing situations. The sample areas contained a wide range of different sizes and types of association (Table 1.4).

1.21 Within each local authority area the research comprised three main strands:

a) structured interviews with the staff of a sample of associations, the local authority, and the regional office of the Housing Corporation; backed up by the collection of reports and other relevant material from the organisations visited.

b) the collection and analysis of statistical information relating to new applicants to associations and to the local authority, over a six month period while the study was in progress, together with nalysis of the NFHA CORE returns from the sample associations, and

c) group and in-depth interviews with a small number of new applicants carried out by British Market Research Bureau (BMRB) to find out what applicants thought about the way associations and local authorities offer their services and allocate their properties.

The interviews

1.22 The response from associations invited to participate in the survey was excellent; only two felt unable to assist. Interviews were carried out between October 1990 and June 1991. Respondents within the housing associations were for the most part regional or area housing managers with allocations officers sometimes also present. At the Housing Corporation's regional offices interviews were conducted with area managers whose responsibilities covered the case study areas, while at the local authorities, interviews were typically held with senior staff responsible for allocations and lettings.

1.23 Although respondents in the housing associations were, as far as possible, asked to relate their comments to the position as it affected the case study areas, most had experience over a much wider area and it was ofen clear that their replies were to some extent influenced by this broader perspective.

1.24 Within each case study area, the sample of associations was chosen from information supplied by the Housing Corporation. All associations with housing stock in the case study area were ranked in order of the number of dwellings they managed in that area. Those with largest stock were chosen with a cut off point being taken when approximately 80 per cent of the housing association stock was covered. It can be seen from Table 1.2 that this objective was very closely achieved. The method of selection meant that only the very smallest associations in each area were excluded.

Table 1.2 **Coverage of housing association activity achieved from sample of associations participating**

	Housing Association Stock April 1990			Lettings Oct 1990 - Mar 1991		
	All HAs in area	Sample HAs	% in Sample	All HAs in area	Sample HAs	% in Sample
Bolton	3,400	3,100	91	183	158	86
Bromley	4,500	3,400	76	175	118	67
Camden	6,000	4,600	77	164	153	93
Derby	4,200	3,200	76	447	343	77
Exeter	1,700	1,400	82	97	72	74
Leeds	8,500	7,500	88	460	349	76
Total	28,300	23,200	82	1,526	1,193	78

Sources: Housing stock - Local Authorities and Participating Housing Associations; Lettings - NFHA CORE Returns.

1.25 A further check on the coverage of the sample can be seen by comparing the number of lettings made by participating associations with those not included in the study. This shows that although the proportion of lettings in the sample was generally very high there was a lower proportion than might have been expected in Bromley and to a lesser extent Exeter, Leeds and Derby. Examination of CORE returns suggests that this is due to new schemes being let by one or two associations which either had a small number of existing dwellings in the area (and hence were not included in the sample) or were new to the area. As the number of lettings made over the six month period was small one or two new schemes would have had a large effect. Overall the coverage of housing association lettings achieved through the sample was very high and provides a good insight into the policies and practices of associations in the areas covered.

1.26 A list of the housing associations participating in the study is shown in Table 1.3. Forty five different associations took part ranging from large national organisations such as Anchor Housing Association and North British with over 20,000 dwellings each to small local associations such as Glebe Housing Association and Penge Churches with less than 200 properties. Anchor Housing Association and Sutton Housing Trust were interviewed in three of the case study areas; and Guinness Trust, North British, and Northern Counties Housing Association in two areas. Fifty two interviews were conducted in all.

Table 1.3 **List of housing associations participating in the study**

LEEDS (14)	BROMLEY(12)	BOLTON(9)
Anchor HA	Asra	Anchor HA
Bradford & Northern HA Ltd	Church HA	Collingwood HA
Castle Gate HS Ltd	Family HA	Hanover Housing HA
Harewood HS Ltd	Glebe HA Ltd	Irwell Valley HA Ltd
Headrow Housing Group	Hyde HA Ltd	Moorside HA Ltd
Leeds Federated HA	Kelsey HA Ltd	North British HA Ltd
Leeds Jewish HA Ltd	Keniston HA Ltd	Northern Counties HA Ltd
North British HA Ltd	Moat HS Ltd	Portico HA Ltd
Northern Counties HA Ltd	Penge Churches HA Ltd	Sutton HT
Ridings HA Ltd	Servite Houses Ltd	
Royal British Legion HA Ltd	Shaftesbury Society HA	
Sanctuary HA	South London Family	
Sutton HT		
Yorkshire Metropolitan HA Ltd		
CAMDEN (7)	**DERBY (6)**	**EXETER (4)**
Central London HT	Anchor HA	Devon and Cornwall HA Ltd
Circle 33 HT	Derwent HS Ltd	Devon Community HS Ltd
Community HA Ltd	Sutton HT	Exeter HS Ltd
Humanist HA	The Guinness Trust	The Guinness Trust
Paddington Churches HA Ltd	United Kingdom HT	
St Pancras HA	Walbrook HA Ltd	
The Peabody Trust		

NFHA CORE monitoring returns

1.27 The NFHA runs a continuous monitoring system for all self-contained general needs new lettings and sales made by housing associations in England; this is known as CORE. The NFHA provided tabulations of basic information from these returns for all lettings made by associations in the case study areas (i.e. both participating and non-participating associations) for the period October 1990 - March 1991. This provided a valuable source of information about the characteristics of the dwellings let and the people rehoused by the associations in each case study area. Returns were received from all the associations included in the study in Camden, Derby and Exeter and only one association (with a few lettings) did not provide returns in Bromley. It is unfortunate that in Bolton and Leeds one large general needs association did not send in any returns thus making the figures in these two areas incomplete.

New applicants survey

1.28 All participating associations were asked to complete a short form containing information similar to the CORE returns for each new applicant applying for housing (other than nominations from local authorities) over the period from October 1990 to March 1991. Two problems were experienced with this exercise;

a) there was some non-response because a small number of associations were not able to find the resources to complete the returns, and

b) very low numbers of new applicants were recorded in Bromley and Camden (because associations either did not take direct applicants or their waiting lists were closed) and in Exeter (because there were not many new applicants).

1.29 Local authorities were also asked to complete a similar form for their new applicants for five separate one week periods throughout the period of the study. Camden, Bolton and Leeds did not feel able to complete this part of the exercise because of the demands it would have made upon staff time and because of fears over the confidentiality of information.

Group interviews with applicants

1.30 In order to obtain a consumer perspective on the services provided by both housing associations and local authorities, a number of group discussions led by BMRB were held amongst applicants. The original intention of conducting these interviews in all case study areas had to be modified because of the low number of new applicants in Bromley and Camden. Two group interviews were conducted in Bolton (families and older people), Leeds (singles and families) and Exeter (also singles and families) while in Derby three sessions were held (older people, singles and families). In order to obtain some information from Camden and Bromley in-depth interviews were held with a small number of recent applicants.

1.31 The group interviews were designed to obtain the views and experiences of applicants. The main topics covered included the reasons why people had applied to a housing association, how they had obtained information about associations, their experience of the applications process, and their views about housing associations in comparison with local authorities.

The case study area: descriptions

1.32 Bolton (population 265,000) is part of Greater Manchester. It has the second highest incidence of statutory homelessness in the area and much sub-standard terraced housing. There is a large ethnic minority population and a considerable number of older people. Fourteen associations operate in the town. There are a mix of national associations such as North British, Northern Counties, Sutton, Anchor, and Hanover, Manchester based associations like Deansgate and St. Vincents and local associations such as Moorside and Irwell Valley. Eight associations are actively developing in the area.

1.33 Bromley (population 299,400) is an outer London borough. It is mainly suburban and affluent but with some deprived areas and a rising homelessness problem. A large number of associations (almost 50) operate in the borough but most are very small. The largest is Hyde with 600 properties. The largest associations are mostly based in South London and the southern home counties. Current development activity by associations in the borough is fairly limited. The Borough are planning to transfer their own stock to a newly created housing association.

1.34 Camden (population 183,700) is an inner London borough exhibiting many typical problems of housing stress such as housing shortage, poor quality of stock, and homelessness. It has a high ethnic minority population and a high proportion of single person households. Over 40 associations operate in the borough but, as in Bromley, most are small with only six having over 100 properties. The largest are Circle 33 with 902 dwellings and Paddington Churches with 705.

1.35 Derby (population 216,600) is a major commercial and industrial town in the East Midlands with a high incidence of homelessness, a growing waiting list and much substandard stock. Sixteen housing associations operate in the area, the largest being Walbrook with 1,532 properties and Derwent with 725. Seven of the associations have less than 100 properties.

1.36 Exeter (population 102,300) is a major regional centre in the South West. Its housing problems are not as severe as the other case study areas but it has a growing problem of homelessness and a shortage of rented housing. Only seven associations operate in the City; by far the largest is The Exeter Housing Society with over 800 properties. There are two Devon and Cornwall based associations and also one national association (The Guinness Trust) which has only one estate in the City.

1.37 Leeds (population 711,700) is by far the largest of the case study areas and is the major commercial and industrial centre in West Yorkshire. It has a large number of associations (45) the largest of which is Leeds Federated with 1,642 dwellings. The associations include a mixture of national, regional and local organisations. Leeds Partnership Homes is a consortia of five associations (viz Anchor, Leeds Federated, North British, Ridings, and Sanctuary Spiral) which have formed a non-profit making company which will co-ordinate the provision of new social rented housing in Leeds over the next three years. Some other associations which are not full members of the consortia will operate within its framework.

Table 1.4 **Size distribution of housing associations operating in case study areas (in terms of the number of properties managed by the association in all areas they operate in)**

	Bolton	Bromley	Camden	Derby	Exeter	Leeds	Total *
<1001	1	3	2	0	2	5	13
1001-2500	2	4	2	2	1	2	13
2501-10000	2	5	2	2	1	2	13
>10000 +	3	0	1	3	0	5	6
Total	8	12	7	7	4	14	45

* The total column has been adjusted to allow for associations that were interviewed in more than one case study area.

Source: NFHA Housing Associations Directory and Yearbook 1990/91.

The case study areas compared

1.38 Table 1.4 gives the size distribution of the housing associations operating in the case study areas in terms of their total stock size (in all areas not just the case study areas). As the table shows the sample consisted of a reasonable mix through the size ranges, and there were also some interesting differences between the areas - in Bolton, Derby and Leeds large national organisations (10,000 or more dwellings) were well represented, whereas in Bromley and Camden medium sized associations dominated. In Exeter the associations selected were small to medium locally based organisations (the one large national association only had a small number of dwellings in the City). Most associations in the sample were charitable (see Glossary), all were in Camden but in Leeds six were not, and in Bolton three were not. In the other areas only one association was not charitable.

Table 1.5 **Stock of social housing - case study areas, April 1990**

	Local Authority		Housing Association		Total
	No	%	No	%	
Bolton	24,600	88	3,400	12	28,000
Bromley	12,700	74	4,500	26	17,200
Camden	34,200	85	6,000	15	40,200
Derby	18,100	81	4,200	19	22,300
Exeter	6,900	80	1,700	20	8,600
Leeds	84,700	91	8,500	9	93,200
Total	181,200	86	28,300	14	209,500

Source: The Housing Corporation and participating agencies.

1.39 The stock of housing owned by local authorities and housing associations in the case study areas is shown in Table 1.5. There is a very large stock of social housing in Leeds and 91 per cent of this is local authority owned. Leeds also has numerically the largest number of housing association dwellings of the case study areas. Bromley however, with 26 per cent has the highest proportion of association dwellings followed by Exeter with 20 per cent and Derby with 19 per cent.

1.40 The size distribution of both local authority and housing association dwellings is given in Table 1.6. The most obvious difference between the two sectors is the much higher proportion of one bedroomed properties owned by housing associations - well over a half compared with just over a quarter owned by the local authorities. Exeter associations had the lowest proportion of one bedroomed dwellings (41 per cent) mainly because the largest association, the Exeter Housing Society had a large inter-war estate of three bedroomed properties. Local authorities had a much higher proportion of three bedroomed properties; these amounted to just over a third of all their dwellings.

Table 1.6 **No. of bedrooms in dwelling stock owned by participating associations and local authorities - case study areas, April 1990**

	Bed-sit 1 Bed	2 Bed	3 Bed	4+ Bed	Base
Bolton HAs %	58	26	14	2	3,100
LA %	28	31	38	3	24,600
Bromley HAs %	54	31	11	4	3,400
LA %	32	31	34	3	12,700
Camden HAs %	64	22	11	3	4,600
LA %	40	32	21	6	34,200
Derby HAs %	58	29	12	1	3,200
LA %	24	25	49	1	18,100
Exeter HAs %	41	27	31	2	1,400
LA %	26	32	41	1	6,900
Leeds HAs %	56	30	11	4	7,500
LA %	23	38	34	4	84,700
Total HAs %	57	27	13	3	23,200
LAs %	28	34	35	3	181,200

Source: Participating agencies.

1.41 It was not possible to collect complete information on the proportion of stock owned by associations that were flats, maisonettes or bed-sits although the information which was collected suggested that it was high. The effect of this can be seen in the CORE lettings data shown in Table 1.7, although other factors such as the higher turnover of flats, maisonettes and bed-sits compared with houses will also have played a part. This shows that, on average, over three-quarters of lettings to new tenants were flats etc., and that the proportions were particulary high in Bromley, Camden and Exeter.

Table 1.7 **Lettings to new tenants by property type - case study areas, October 1990 - March 1991**

	Bolton %	Bromley %	Camden %	Derby %	Exeter %	Leeds %	Total %
Flat, maisonette and bed-sit	69	90	97	70	91	78	78
House and other	31	10	3	30	9	22	22
Base	151	122	108	348	74	372	1,175

Source: NFHA CORE Returns.

1.42 Provision for older people has been a traditional role of housing associations and there were several associations operating in the case study areas which specialised in such provision (4 each in Bromley and Leeds, 3 in Bolton, 2 in Camden, and one in each of the other two areas). Table 1.8 shows the proportion of lettings made to people over retirement age; this was particularly high in Bolton, Exeter and Leeds. Sheltered housing (see Glossary) formed a very high proportion of the lettings made to elderly tenants in all the case study areas: the figures being Bolton 80 per cent, Bromley 97 per cent, Camden 92 per cent, Derby 94 per cent, Exeter 96 per cent and Leeds 73 per cent.

***Table 1.8* Lettings to new tenants over retirement age - case study areas, October 1990 - March 1991**

	Bolton	Bromley	Camden	Derby	Exeter	Leeds	Total
	%	%	%	%	%	%	%
Above Retirement Age	48	29	23	15	37	32	28
Below Retirement Age	52	71	77	85	63	68	72
Base	151	121	107	343	73	368	1,163

Source: NFHA CORE Returns.

1.43 An indication of the level of recent development activity in the case study areas can be seen from Table 1.9. This shows that new lets (i.e. properties let for the first time in new, rehabilitated or acquired properties) ranged from just under a third in Bolton, Camden and Derby, to 20 per cent in Bromley and Exeter and 15 per cent in Leeds.

***Table 1.9* Lettings to new tenants by letting type - case study areas, October 1990 - March 1991**

	Bolton	Bromley	Camden	Derby	Exeter	Leeds	Total
	%	%	%	%	%	%	%
New let	32	20	31	31	20	15	24
Relet	68	80	69	69	80	85	76
Base	150	122	107	348	74	371	1,172

Source: NFHA CORE Returns.

How typical are the case study areas?

1.44 Most of the housing associations interviewed operated in more than one local authority and the vast majority utilise the same allocations policies and practices in all areas they operate in. This means that as far as direct lettings are concerned (i.e. all those apart from nominations) the findings are relevant to a much wider area.

1.45 It is useful to compare the size of the associations interviewed (in terms of all their properties) with the national size distribution (Table 1.10).

Table 1.10 **Size of housing associations (no. of dwellings owned) - sample associations and England, 1990**

	Sample Associations				England			
	No of associations		Stock owned		No of associations		Stock owned	
	No	%	No (000)	%	No	%	No (000)	%
< 250	3	7	0.5	0	1,917	88	49.7	9
251 - 1,000	10	22	6.4	2	138	6	74.8	13
1001 - 2,500	13	29	22.7	12	81	4	116.9	21
2,501 - 10,000	13	29	75.8	40	42	2	197.6	35
Over 10,000	6	13	88.9	46	8	0	129.3	23
Total	45	100	194.3	100	2,186	100	568.3	100

Source: Sample associations and Housing Corporation.

1.46 Overall the associations interviewed owned 194,300 dwellings of the 568,300 dwellings owned by all associations in England (34 per cent). As expected, the sample is heavily weighted towards the larger associations, but this is also true of England where a very high proportion of the total housing association stock is owned by the larger associations. Six out of the eight large national associations were included in the study and 13 out of the 42 medium sized associations with between 2,501 and 10,000 dwellings.

1.47 A further indicator of the representativeness of the sample of areas chosen for the study is given in Table 1.11. This table compares NFHA CORE lettings data and case study data with respect to household types. Although the time periods do not exactly coincide, the table indicates that there is little difference between the two.

Table 1.11 **Comparison of lettings (including transfers) by household type - case study areas (October 1990 - March 1991) and England (October - December 1990)**

	Case Study Areas %	England %
One elderly person	21	21
Two elderly people	8	8
One adult	30	27
Two adults	10	9
Single parent family	17	17
Other families with children	13	15
Other	1	2
Base	1,458	13,891

Source: NFHA CORE Returns.

1.48 The systems used by local authorities and housing associations to organise nominations clearly relate in a much more specific way to the study areas. However, when the proportion of new lettings made to nominees between October 1990 and March 1991 in the case study areas was compared with the CORE figure for England (last quarter 1990) the proportions were very close - 42 per cent for the case study areas and 41 per cent for England. This does suggest that the result of the process, if not the process itself, was similar in the case study areas to the national pattern.

Summary

1.49 Housing association activity is characterised by its variety and the case study areas were selected to try to encompass this variety. The areas were not specifically chosen to be representative of all areas. It is clear, however, from the above analysis that the case study areas represent a valid cross-section of housing association activities with some similarities and some differences. This is a useful basis from which to describe how properties are reallocated and how associations fit into the wider housing scene.

Chapter 2 Applying for housing through housing associations

Introduction

2.1 This chapter deals with the processes of selecting households for access to rehousing through housing associations. Association lettings come from a number of different sources:

- Direct applications and waiting lists;
- Transfers and exchanges;
- Referral agencies;
- Mobility schemes and reciprocal arrangements; and
- Local authority nominations.

2.2 Housing associations are expected to provide accommodation for those who are inadequately housed or homeless and whose needs cannot be met, either at all or at prices within their means, elsewhere in the local housing market. However, within the broad framework set out by the Tenants' Guarantee (see Glossary) associations are free to determine their own policy objectives.

2.3 In their report "Standards for Housing Management" (NFHA, 1987) the National Federation of Housing Associations recommended that all associations should have clear and specific objectives in at least the following three areas of selection and allocation:

a) the types of housing need that the associations aim to meet;

b) that lettings and allocations will be done fairly and according to the relevant law; and

c) that they will be done as quickly and efficiently as possible in the best interests of both the applicants and the use of the properties.

2.4 Whilst recognising the autonomy and independence of individual associations, the Housing Corporation in their guide "Performance Expectations" (Housing Corporation, 1989, see Glossary) indicate that they expect associations to provide open and fair access to housing, aimed at those in serious housing need. More specifically in deciding on their priority needs and client groups they are expected to be locally responsive and to take account of the following:

- Local Housing Needs;
- Helping with Statutory Homeless;
- Special Housing Needs;
- Housing Needs of Ethnic Minorities;
- Provision by Other Bodies;
- Constitutional Requirements; and
- Type of Accommodation Provided.

In addition it is anticipated that associations will be responsive to changing housing needs and priorities through both their initial allocations and transfers.

2.5 The aims of this chapter and the next are as follows:

(a) to consider the various means of access to housing association properties;

(b) to examine who may apply, and who does apply, for housing association accommodation;

(c) to examine the different ways in which associations operate waiting list arrangements;

(d) to consider how associations prioritise applicants in making allocations, and examine the outcomes in terms of who is being housed;

(e) to examine the arrangements by which associations use Referral Agencies to obtain new applicants and tenants;

(f) to consider how associations deal with requests for transfers from their existing tenants and the use which is made of national mobility schemes (HOMES); and

(g) finally, to consider the arrangements which associations make for setting targets, monitoring and performance review in relation to selection and allocation.

The issue of local authority nomination arrangements is dealt with separately in chapter 4.

2.6 The issues outlined above are dealt with by reference to the interviews conducted in each of the six local authority areas studied, the analysis of new applicants data collected from associations in four areas (Bolton, Derby, Exeter and Leeds, but not Bromley and Camden, because of the low level of direct applications in these localities and the relatively high levels of local authority nominations and direct referrals to new tenancies) and the analysis of new lettings data in the six local authorities using information provided through the CORE returns from participating associations.

The application process and waiting lists

Who may apply?

2.7 All the associations interviewed stressed that their objective was to provide housing for those in need, although the associations interviewed in the six areas catered for a wide range of different housing needs.

2.8 Some associations provided a range of both general family and special needs accommodation, including housing for the physically and the mentally handicapped and mentally ill. Others, (e.g. Anchor, Liversage Trust) provide accommodation exclusively for the elderly.

2.9 In determining what is housing need, most associations stressed similar categories including the following:

- homeless households (though many associations stressed that statutorily homeless people would only be rehoused via local authority nominations);
- those threatened by homelessness;

- families prevented from living together through lack of suitable accommodation;
- those without security of tenure;
- those suffering from a lack of basic amenities and/or serious disrepair;
- people with medical problems;
- those with unsuitable present accommodation; and
- those with certain defined requirements such as a need to be nearer to present employment or elderly relatives.

2.10 Housing associations have a duty to assist local authorities to meet their specific responsibility for homelessness, usually through nomination arrangements. Under the Housing Act 1985 (s.72) local authorities may require associations to provide reasonable assistance in meeting these statutory responsibilities.

2.11 However, the question of defining homelessness is complex. Since this research was undertaken the NFHA have revised their CORE system new lettings log and asked associations to indicate whether households were homeless (based upon the statutory definition) at the time of rehousing. This information is now disaggregated into four categories; statutory homeless, non-statutorily homeless (non priority homeless), not homeless or threatened with homelessness. This last category covers those cases where households will not become homeless within 28 days but would become statutorily homeless in due course.

2.12 Unfortunately, during the six months that new lettings were monitored for this research, this categorisation was unavailable and associations were simply asked to provide the main immediate reason for rehousing.

Information and advertising

2.13 In terms of who may apply for rehousing, most associations interviewed did not have any blanket restriction policies. However, some associations stated that they deliberately excluded certain categories of applicant. In Exeter, for example, one association does not consider applications from single people under 40; another said that owner-occupiers would not be considered unless they had particular problems (e.g. impending mortgage foreclosure). Similar restrictions were noted in Bromley, together with households not considered to be in housing need and existing tenants of the local authority or housing associations (except under nomination arrangements or mobility schemes).

2.14 Obviously those associations catering specifically for the elderly do have restrictive criteria. For example, Humanist operating in Camden, restricts eligibility to "persons over 60 years old who are capable of living independently in a self-contained flat, possibly with the assistance of family or friends and domiciliary services. They must either already live in the area or have strong reasons for wishing to move into the area". Central London Housing Trust use similar criteria.

2.15 Some associations (in particular the charitable trusts) place an income/savings limit on prospective tenants in order to ensure that accommodation is provided to those with low financial means. The Sutton

Housing Trust, for example, with estates in Bolton, Derby and Leeds only consider applicants provided they do not have gross incomes in excess of the limits set out below:

Household Size	Weekly Income £	Annual Income £
One person	168	8,770
Two persons	243	12,685
Three persons	248	12,946
Four persons	254	13,259
Five persons	261	13,624

In addition, applicants under 60 years of age with capital assets in excess of £20,000 are not considered or applicants over 60 with capital in excess of £30,000. These criteria, which are set annually by the Trustees, relate to the charitable objective of the Trust which is to provide relief to those in conditions of housing need who are on low incomes.

2.16 Most associations interviewed stressed the enormous size of the demand for their properties and did not widely advertise the services they offer, although all provide explanatory leaflets about their objectives and allocation policies, who may apply to them for rehousing and (in some cases) details of the type and location of properties which they manage.

2.17 In Bolton, for example, it was generally felt that there was a lack of information about associations either from the associations themselves or the local council. One association commented that they were not very "applicant oriented". They felt they provided a wealth of information for their tenants - but very little for new applicants.

2.18 In some areas the local authority have worked together with local housing associations to provide Housing Association Directories (e.g. Derby, Leeds). In Exeter the City Council and associations were jointly working on a leaflet which will provide information about all the associations working in the area. Many associations expressed the view that such directories would help them in reaching those households in the greatest need, although there was some concern that such documents are difficult to keep up-to-date. One option might be to consider producing such information at a local authority level in loose-leaf format.

2.19 In Derby, as well as producing a booklet detailing the names and addresses of all housing associations who have properties for rent in the City, the location of schemes and a brief description of the type of property, the council is also publicising housing associations through its regular tenants' newsletter in order to attract council tenants seeking a transfer. There is also a possibility that associations may hold surgeries in Derby's "Property Shop" in order to attract more people to housing associations.

2.20 However, there were also concerns that by advertising their services associations were in danger of raising false expectations. This was particularly so in Bromley where most associations had leaflets or handouts which could be given to applicants once they had found their way into the system and which explained their allocation policies and practices - but produced nothing specifically designed to attract applicants.

2.21 Associations placed considerable emphasis upon word-of-mouth as the means by which applicants got to know them. Several associations explained that because they were long established they tended to be well known in their traditional areas of operation. Leeds Jewish Housing Association, for example, had widely publicised its activities amongst the Jewish community, although it recognised that because of its limited housing stock (only 374 units in management) it did not find it easy to respond effectively to immediate and emergency needs.

2.22 In some areas information for applicants has been translated into minority group languages. In Leeds, for example, (where 18 per cent of households are from ethnic minority groups) many associations had their lettings policies, application forms, general publicity material and scheme specific information translated into minority languages (e.g. Urdu, Hindi, Gujerati and Punjabi). Leeds Federated, the largest association in Leeds, indicated that it worked closely with the local Community Relations Council and that locally they were well known amongst the ethnic minority population. Anchor, however, expressed the view that they found difficulty in attracting applications from minority groups, particularly those of Asian and Afro Caribbean origin. Partly they believe they are unable to respond to the needs of the extended family, but feel that this may be a generational problem - and in future they expect to house more households from the ethnic minority communities. The association has also built up close links with Unity, the black association operating in the Chapletown area of Leeds and with the United Caribbean Association.

2.23 In Exeter leaflets have not been translated into minority language and no special measures have been adopted to encourage ethnic minority applicants. Most associations felt that there was no demand for such a service in Exeter.

Assessing applications

2.24 Outside of the two London Boroughs most associations kept a waiting list or housing register of direct applicants (and in some cases local authority nominees as well), often with a separate list for each scheme or property type.

2.25 In many cases, as indicated above, there were few restrictions on the eligibility of households to apply for housing association accommodation. However, in general, housing associations, like local authorities, receive far more enquiries for housing than they have accommodation available, and therefore may not accept all applicants on to waiting lists. Sanctuary Housing Association, for example, have an open waiting list but operate a points threshold for entry. Similarly, the Ridings (Leeds) attempts to limit the number of registered applicants to those for whom there is a realistic prospect of rehousing. They indicate to applicants accepted on to their waiting list that they aim to be able to assist them with accommodation within a year.

2.26 From time to time associations with "open" waiting lists considered closing them because of high levels of demand. For example, Walbrook (Derby) took the unprecedented step (for them) of closing their list from 1st August-30th November 1989, the only exceptions being for council nominees and those seeking wheelchair housing. However, the fall in the level of applications during 1989-90 was not as great as anticipated.

2.27 It is recognised that for an association to operate an open waiting list may be very time consuming. However, in order not to exclude those in housing need from applying for rehousing, it may be preferable to allow all to apply but then to apply an initial sift and for associations to accept only those who have some prospect of being rehoused within a realistic period of time.

2.28 It may be appropriate for associations to restrict the size of active waiting lists in relation to the anticipated flow of vacancies and to set thresholds for different types of housing and for different estates. In order to avoid unduly lengthy waiting lists, where applicants have little or no hope of being offered accommodation of their choice (i.e. in a particular area of on a specific estate), they may be invited to apply for alternative lower demand accommodation. Applicants who are not accepted may be advised to reapply at a later date or if their circumstances change.

2.29 Most associations write to unsuccessful applicants to inform them of the result of the application they have made. Many give further information to those who they cannot help directly about alternatives they may try (e.g. the council, other associations, low cost home ownership options etc.).

2.30 Whilst outside of London most of the associations interviewed kept waiting lists which were usually open (though with some having closed lists for particular categories of applicants or for specific schemes) the situation was rather different in our two London case studies.

2.31 In Bromley only six of the associations interviewed operated a waiting list (Church, Glebe, Hyde, Moat, Servite and Shaftesbury). These associations indicated that they had to adopt some objective means of keeping the length of the list realistic. This has been most commonly achieved by closing the list to further applicants once there is little prospect of rehousing within a year to eighteen months. One association, for example, closed its lists once they exceeded 10 per cent of the number of units in a particular scheme.

2.32 At the time of the study those associations in Bromley with waiting lists had closed most of them to new applicants, with the exception of sheltered housing schemes where associations reported that the position was much easier.

2.33 In Camden five of the seven associations interviewed no longer operated a waiting list. Paddington Churches closed its list 19 years ago and now takes its tenants exclusively via local authority nominations or referral agencies. St Pancras, Circle 33, Community Housing and Central London Housing Trust also have no official list, although the last of these maintains a record of needy persons and advises people to seek nomination through the local authority. Circle 33 also accepts direct applications to their sheltered units and to a scheme for single Bengalis.

2.34 Of the two associations which do maintain a waiting list, Humanist has not reviewed its list recently. The Peabody Trust is the only association interviewed in relation to Camden which operates a traditional waiting list and this is now restricted to bedsits and one bedroom accommodation, with an upper limit of 250 applicants.

2.35 In general, where waiting list are maintained by housing associations they do not give an accurate picture of the level of housing need. In many instances there will be applicants on the list of who are no longer seeking rehousing. Whilst some associations have not reviewed their waiting lists for some time, others expect applicants to re-register on a regular basis. Sutton

Housing Trust, for example, require applicants to re-register every year whilst Headrow (Leeds) requires all applicants not rehoused by them within six months to do the same. A number of associations were unable to indicate the precise number of applicants on their waiting lists and recognised that it was an overestimate of the true level of demand for their housing.

2.36 In some cases the waiting lists of associations do represent double counting (or more) in so far as some applicants may be on several lists (for vacancies in different schemes or different areas). In addition, waiting lists may include a pool of council nominees, who will also be registered on the local authority's own housing register. Finally, it was clear that some applicants were (very sensibly) registering their housing need with several associations as well as the local council, in order to maximise their prospects of rehousing.

2.37 In order to manage more effectively the needs and demands for social rented housing there is a strong case for a centrally administered common applicants register for each local authority district. This is discussed further in chapter five.

2.38 This section of chapter two has dealt with the issues of the application process and waiting list arrangements. It has considered who is eligible to apply to housing associations and how applications are dealt with. However, it is also important to look at who does apply and this is addressed in the next section.

Who applies for housing association accommodation ?

2.39 This section examines what type of households applied to housing associations for rehousing in the case study areas during a six month period from 1st November 1990 to 30th April 1991. Information was provided by associations on a New Applicants Log (appendix D) designed to be broadly compatible with the New Lettings Form used by the NFHA in the CORE analysis.

2.40 The survey was designed to include all direct applications to associations during the study period regardless of whether the applicants were accepted on to the waiting list, a deferred list, or not accepted at all. However, the survey excluded existing tenants requesting a transfer or who were being decanted between the associations' properties.

2.41 As noted in the previous section the response to this element of the study varied. Not all associations kept waiting lists or accept applications on a regular basis. In many instances this depended on the number of newly developed houses becoming available to let and on the numbers of existing tenants who left. Waiting lists, if they existed at all, were only open for limited periods of time. Alternatively, applications were only accepted from certain households.

2.42 In the light of a very low level of new direct applications to associations in both Bromley and Camden it was not possible to include these two areas in the analysis of who applies for housing association accommodation. However, in the other four local authorities details were received of almost 4,000 new applications during the study period.

2.43 Over half (52 per cent) of these were received from 12 associations in Leeds, a further 27 per cent from 3 associations in Derby, 16 per cent from

6 associations in Bolton and 5 per cent from 4 associations in Exeter. The results of this part of the study are set out below.

2.44 Table 2.1 shows the household typology of the applicants in each of the four case study areas. The highest number of applications came from non-pensionable adult-only households, who accounted overall for almost a third (32 per cent) of all applicants. However, this group only accounted for about a quarter of applicants in both Exeter and Bolton. In Exeter the largest proportion of new applicants came from single person elderly households (26 per cent) whilst in Bolton single parent households (with one or two children) were almost as significant as single adults in making application for association accommodation. Overall, small single parent family households were the second largest group of new applicants after single adults.

2.45 Interestingly, the elderly were not a major source of new direct applicants, except in Exeter. Overall, they accounted for 16 per cent of applicants, with single elderly applicants being almost twice as great as elderly couples. However in Exeter the elderly accounted for over 40 per cent of new applicants.

2.46 A high proportion of the applications from single adults came from those in younger age groups. In Leeds 49 per cent of single adults were aged 24 or less and a further 24 per cent between 25 and 31 years old. A similar picture emerges in Derby where the comparable figures were 52 per cent (16-24) and 25 per cent (25-31). However, the concentration amongst younger singles was less in Bolton, where over two fifths of single applicants (41 per cent) were aged 32-59.

Table 2.1 **New applicants to housing associations: household type by local authority area**

	Bolton %	Derby %	Exeter %	Leeds %	Total %
Single Elderly	10	5	27	11	10
Elderly Couple	5	3	14	6	6
Single Adult	26	35	26	33	32
Adult Couple	12	19	16	14	15
3 or more Adults	3	1	1	2	2
2 or more Adults and 1/2 children	13	13	9	12	12
2 or more Adults and 3 or more children	4	2	2	3	3
1 Adult and 1/2 children	26	17	6	17	18
1 Adult and 3 or more children	3	4	1	3	3
Base No.	617	1,079	187	2,041	3,924

Source: New Applicants Survey.

2.47 Over 80 per cent of applicants were already established as independent households at the time of application. Of these, 85 per cent were continuing households and the remaining 15 per cent separating.

2.48 Information on ethnic origin was provided in respect of almost 90 per cent of cases. As table 2.2 indicates over 87 per cent of these applications were received from those of White European origin. However, 1 in 20 applicants were Black British, with particular concentrations in Leeds (8 per cent of applicants) and Derby (4 per cent of applicants). Black Asian applicants represented only 3 per cent of the total, and were most significant in Bolton (4 per cent of applicants).

2.49 In Leeds applications from those of Black British origin were concentrated amongst single adults (45 per cent) and single parent small households (27 per cent). A similar picture emerged in Derby where over half of all applications from Black British applicants (55 per cent) were from single adults whilst a further 17 per cent came from single parent small families.

2.50 In Bolton amongst Black Asian applicants the picture was a little different. A third of this group were single parent small families, a further 24 per cent two adults and one or two children, and 14 per cent adult couples. Only 10 per cent were single adults of non pensionable age.

Table 2.2 **New applicants to housing associations: ethnic origin by local authority area**

	Bolton %	Derby %	Exeter %	Leeds %	Total %
Black Asian	4	3	1	3	3
Black Caribbean	---	3	---	2	2
Black African	1	1	---	1	1
White European	94	87	98	84	87
Black British	1	4	1	8	5
Other	1	3	1	2	2
Base No.	573	1,063	189	1,720	3,545

Source: New Applicants Survey.

2.51 The elderly were particulary poorly represented amongst ethnic minority group applicants. In Bolton and Exeter there were no applications during the survey period from elderly minorities, whilst in Leeds only 3 per cent of the Black British applicants were elderly and in Derby the comparable figure was only 5 per cent. However, although the number of applicants was relatively small, over 13 per cent of the Black Asian applicants in Derby were elderly.

2.52 Table 2.3 shows the economic status of applicants (head of household). Almost a third of the applicants (33 per cent) were in full-time employment, whilst a further 4 percent were working part-time (defined as less than 30 hours per week). There was a general level of consistency across all four case study areas in terms of those in employment.

Table 2.3 **New applicants to housing associations: economic status by local authority area**

Bolton	Derby	Exeter	Leeds	Total	
	%	%	%	%	%
Working Full-Time	32	36	31	31	33
Working Part-Time	7	2	4	5	4
Registered Unemployed	24	26	15	34	29
Retired	15	8	36	16	15
At Home/Not seeking work	17	21	5	7	12
Permanently Sick/Disabled	3	4	7	3	4
In Full-Time Education	2	2	---	1	2
Other	2	2	---	1	2
Base No.	592	1,016	188	1,926	3,722

Source : New Applicants Survey.

2.53 Almost 3 in 10 of the applicants were registered unemployed. However, if the elderly and those not seeking work or permanently sick or disabled are excluded then the employment rate amongst applicants (i.e. the proportion of the economically active who were out of work) was significantly higher, affecting more than 42 per cent of economically active applicants (46 per cent in Leeds, but only 29 per cent in Exeter)

2.54 Unemployment was particulary high amongst single adult applicants. In both Leeds and Derby almost 2 in every 5 of these applicants were unemployed whilst the comparable figures in Bolton and Exeter were 33 per cent and 29 per cent respectively.

2.55 Table 2.4 shows the tenure of applicants in their present accommodation. For all but elderly people, the most common form of accommodation was either sharing with family/friends (36 per cent) or renting from a private landlord (22 per cent). However, a significant number of new applicants were owner-occupiers (15 per cent overall and 23 per cent in Bolton) or renting from the council or housing association (16 per cent).

2.56 In Bolton half of single adults were living with family/friends. The comparable figures in Derby and Leeds were 48 per cent and 45 per cent respectively and for Exeter 30 per cent, where 2 in every 5 single adult applicants were renting privately.

2.57 By way of comparison, 58 per cent of single elderly applicants in Bolton and 64 per cent of elderly couples were owner occupiers. In Leeds over 40 per cent of each of these groups owned their own homes, whilst in Derby a third of single elderly applicants and 58 per cent of elderly couples were owner-occupiers. In Exeter the comparable figures were 16 and 32 per cent.

2.58 14 per cent of new applicants in Leeds were existing council tenants. In terms of household type 27 per cent of single elderly applicants, 29 per cent of elderly couple applicants and 19 per cent of family household applicants in Leeds were renting from the local authority.

Table 2.4 **New applicants to housing associations: present tenure by local authority area**

	Bolton %	Derby %	Exeter %	Leeds %	Total %
Renting - Council	10	9	8	14	12
Renting - Housing Association	3	2	12	5	4
Renting - Private Landlord	16	26	36	20	22
Owned/Buying	23	14	14	13	15
With Family/ Friends	44	37	20	35	36
In Bed and Breakfast	1	2	2	---	1
In Hostel	3	5	2	8	6
In Institution	---	2	---	---	1
Other	2	3	5	3	3
Base No.	649	1,079	187	2,052	3,967

Source : New Applicants Survey.

Income

2.59 Table 2.5 shows the total net weekly household income of the applicants in the study. Well over half (58 per cent) of all applicants had a net weekly household income of under £100 per week. However, at the other end of the spectrum, over 9 per cent of applicants had a weekly household income in excess of £200 (13 per cent in Derby and 17 per cent in Exeter).

2.60 In Leeds 71 per cent of single adults had net weekly incomes of below £100. The comparable figures in the other case study areas were 63 per cent in Derby, 56 per cent in Exeter, and 55 per cent in Bolton.

2.61 70 per cent of elderly person households had net weekly household incomes of less than £100 per week, ranging from 61 per cent in Bolton to 73 per cent in Leeds.

2.62 Of those applicants with an income in excess of £200 per week, 86 per cent were cases where the head of household was in full-time employment. Almost half (46 per cent) of such applicants were adult couples whilst a further 22 per cent were small families (two or more adults plus 1 or 2 children) and 11 per cent single adults of non pensionable age.

2.63 Half of all applicants, ranging from 38 per cent in Exeter to 57 per cent in Derby, had their household income wholly derived from state benefits, whilst a further 21 per cent had incomes in part from the state. Associations estimated that 70 per cent of applicants would be likely to qualify for housing benefit when rehoused.

Table 2.5 **New applicants to housing associations: net weekly household income by local authority area**

	Bolton	Derby	Exeter	Leeds	Total
	%	%	%	%	%
Up to £39.99	11	12	8	16	13
£40 - £59.99	16	13	17	19	17
£60 - £79.99	18	17	13	16	16
£80 - £99.99	13	9	13	11	11
£100 - £119.99	13	11	7	10	10
£120 - £139.99	12	9	9	8	9
£140 - £159.99	8	11	8	6	8
£160 - £179.99	5	4	5	4	4
£180 - £199.99	2	3	4	2	3
£200 and over	3	13	18	9	9
Base No.	515	695	168	1,658	3,036

Source: New Applicants Survey.

2.64 Table 2.6 shows the reason given by applicants for seeking rehousing through housing associations. Over a quarter (26 per cent) indicated that they were homeless or potentially homeless. The next most often cited reasons were overcrowding (18 per cent of cases), the need for independence (12 per cent) and health/medical reasons (11 per cent).

2.65 Associations indicated for almost 90 per cent of applicants whether or not they were already on the local authority's waiting list. Two thirds were at the time of their application to associations.

2.66 Associations were also asked to indicate whether or not applicants were already on the waiting list of another association. 41 per cent of those applicants for whom information was available (83 per cent of all applicants) were registered on at least one other association's waiting list.

2.67 Finally, associations indicated that 68 per cent of the applications received would be accepted on to the waiting list. This ranged from over 95 per cent in Derby to just under 50 per cent in Bolton. However, as was explained at the beginning of this section, this is partly a function of how individual associations manage their waiting lists.

Table 2.6 **New applicants to housing associations: reasons for seeking rehousing by local authority area**

	Bolton %	Derby %	Exeter %	Leeds %	Total %
Overcrowding	27	17	12	17	18
Under-Occupation	1	2	1	3	2
Poor Housing	4	9	12	6	7
Health/Medical	14	9	13	12	11
Need for Sheltered Housing	1	3	6	4	3
Nearer Family	2	4	13	5	5
Need Independence	10	17	14	10	12
Relationship - Breakdown	6	11	5	6	9
Leaving Temporary Accommodation	1	5	2	2	5
Homeless/Potentially Homeless	21	32	25	25	26
Financial Problems	9	13	10	5	8
Harassment	3	4	1	4	3
Employment	1	2	3	2	2
Social Needs	8	12	10	7	9
Domestic Violence	1	2	1	2	2
Other	2	2	1	2	2
Not Known	3	2	2	10	6
Base No.	652	1,083	192	2,044	3,971

Note: Column percentages do not total to 100. Column figures represent number of responses as a percentage of number cases (i.e. 27% of applicants in Bolton specified overcrowding as a reason for seeking rehousing).

Source: New Applicants Survey.

Summary

2.68 This chapter has been concerned with applications to associations for housing. It has indicated the variations in the practices adopted by associations and in the profile of applicants.

2.69 All associations have their own allocation policies set within the context of corporation and NFHA guidelines. The focus on meeting housing need was universal albeit that there were different emphases in terms of priority given to particular groups.

2.70 Some associations did seek to make best use of their properties by restricting who could apply. Most did not advertise their services although all provided explanatory leaflets about the association and its properties. These were often in a variety of languages.

2.71 Outside of London, most associations kept open waiting lists although some had closed them temporarily. Waiting lists were felt to give a poor picture of local need.

2.72 Nearly half of all applicants to case study associations outside of London were non-pensionable adult only households (49 per cent). A further 16 per cent of applicants were elderly person households. Single parent and two parent households with children made up 36 per cent of applicants (21 per cent and 15 per cent respectively).

2.73 13 per cent of applicants were non-white. 37 per cent were employed (full/part-time). 57 per cent of applicants had household incomes of less than £100 per week.

2.74 Over a quarter of applicants were seeking housing because they were homeless (or threatened with homelessness). Two thirds of all applicants were also on the local authority waiting list. Over a third of all applicants were on the waiting list of another association.

Chapter 3 Allocation policies and practices

Introduction

3.1 Housing Associations operating in each of the six case study areas, in common with associations throughout the country, have a general policy of housing those in the greatest need. Their success in achieving this has been highlighted in recent research conducted for the Department (DoE, 1991).

3.2 As illustrated in chapter 2, housing associations receive far more applications for rehousing than they have accommodation available for letting, and therefore seek to establish fair and practical methods for deciding who gets rehoused.

Policy and practice general context

3.3 There was a good deal of consistency between associations in terms of the factors which are taken into account in assessing need for rehousing. These included:-

- Suitability of present accommodation (in terms of its size, condition, location, access to basic amenities etc).
- Security of existing accommodation.
- Applicants' ability to cope with their existing housing conditions (in terms of factors affecting the physical or mental well-being of the applicant or their family).
- Other personal circumstances of the applicant (family relationships, financial difficulties etc).
- The length of time for which the applicant has had to contend with inadequate housing.

This reflects the advice given by the Housing Corporation.

3.4 In most cases applicants to housing associations are required to complete an application form and direct applicants are then assessed according to either a points system or a priority group category.

3.5 Needs based points systems may give points for a number of factors; e.g. overcrowding, underoccupation, lack of facilities, sharing, property condition (disrepair), current housing situation, medical/social factors, availability of alternative accommodation, families living above first floor level etc. In some instances negative points are applied to applicants who are perceived as having other possible housing opportunities to them (as a result of savings, income level, ability to obtain a mortgage etc).

3.6 Similar factors to those outlined above are likely to determine into which priority group applicants are placed, where this is the system used to determine priorities between applicants. For example, the Ridings Housing Association in Leeds indicate that they give priority to the following types of housing need.

- Homelessness or the threat of homelessness.
- Lack of permanent or secure accommodation.
- Health problems caused by housing conditions.
- Violence within the home or harassment.
- Lack of amenities or inadequate property condition.

3.7 A number of associations expressed the view that points systems and priority group assessments were flawed, and felt that applications were best judged on merit of each case by officers. It was felt that individual applications needed to be assessed in relation to individual vacancies because only then could the competing needs of different applicants be fully considered in respect of their suitability for a specific vacancy. However, it must be recognised that different types of applicant, who may each be in high priority, may have quite different housing needs (e.g. a homeless family compared with a family subjected to harassment.

3.8 Prior to allocation it is usual for associations to make a home visit to applicants to check that the information recorded is correct and their circumstances have not changed.

Housing association lettings

3.9 In this section the characteristics of households allocated a dwelling by all associations in the case study areas during the period 1st October 1990-31st March 1991 are examined. The data is drawn from the NFHA CORE returns covering this six month period. However, it should be noted that the analysis EXCLUDES lettings made as a result of transfers within the housing stock of individual associations.

3.10 Of the remaining allocations almost a quarter (24 per cent) were first lettings, ranging from 15 per cent in Leeds to 32 per cent in Bolton. Two thirds of lettings were of purpose built properties, ranging from 33 per cent in Camden to 91 per cent in Exeter.

Table 3.1 **Size of properties (no. of bedrooms) let - case study areas**

	Bolton %	Bromley %	Camden %	Derby %	Exeter %	Leeds %	Total
1 Bedroom	67	65	58	61	86	72	67
2 Bedrooms	25	33	30	21	8	18	22
3 Bedrooms	8	2	12	18	5	10	11
Base	151	122	108	348	74	372	1,175

Source: NFHA CORE Returns.

In all six case study areas a majority of the lettings made were of small dwellings (two thirds were one bedroom properties).

3.11 Almost a quarter (24 per cent) of lettings were of sheltered accommodation, ranging from 16 per cent in Derby to 38 per cent in Bolton. 21 per cent of the lettings were of dwellings designed to mobility standard and 7 per cent to wheelchair standard.

3.12 Table 3.2 shows the origin of tenants. Almost half (46 per cent) of the new lettings were made to direct applicants, with a majority in Bolton, Derby, Exeter and Leeds. However, less than a quarter of new lettings in Bromley were made as a result of direct applicants and less than 1 in 10 in Camden.

3.13 In comparison, 72 per cent of all lettings were made to local authority nominees in Camden and 55 per cent in Bromley. In the remaining four case study authorities the proportion ranged from 34-39 per cent. The issue of nominations is discussed fully in chapter four, but these figures illustrate that it was only in the two London boroughs studied that the 50 per cent target for nominations was achieved.

3.14 A minority of new lettings were made as a results of referrals from statutory or voluntary agencies, with this being most significant in Bromley. In this authority four associations (Family, Keniston, Penge, and South London Family) had formal systems in operation whereby they worked closely with referral agencies. Associations expected the agencies to make a preliminary assessment of need and only to refer those who reached certain levels. Usually the referral agencies were asked for a nomination around the time a vacancy was anticipated. Similar arrangements operated in five of the associations working in Camden.

Table 3.2 **New lettings by housing associations: source of referral by local authority area**

	Bolton %	Bromley %	Camden %	Derby %	Exeter %	Leeds %	Total %
LocalAuthority Nomination	39	55	72	37	34	36	42
Statutory Agency	1	---	1	8	---	2	3
Voluntary Agency	2	13	7	1	1	4	4
Direct Application	57	24	9	54	56	50	46
Mobility Scheme	---	2	7	---	1	--	1
Transfer from other Association	1	2	2	---	7	1	1
Other	---	3	2	---	---	7	3
Base	150	121	107	342	73	369	1,162

Source: NFHA CORE Data.

3.15 It was evident from the case study research that a diverse group of needs were being catered for. Many of the referral agencies were themselves small and either did not have any accommodation themselves (e.g. advice centres) or could only provide short-term accommodation. Move-on routes into housing associations are critical to their own functioning.

3.16 The referral agencies approached stressed that housing association vacancies were few and far between. Most had written guidelines to assist them in deciding who to refer, and emphasis was often placed upon whether an applicant had any other option available. For example, someone who was likely to qualify as statutory homeless might be referred direct to the local authority rather than a housing association.

3.17 Arrangements for referrals in many ways appear untidy but where associations used referral agencies for allocations they valued their contacts with these organisations who were perceived as being at the "sharp end" of coping with housing need. In general, associations were satisfied that the referral mechanisms did come up with those applicants with the most severe housing needs.

3.18 Only small numbers of new lettings were made as a result of mobility schemes, with Camden (7%) being the only area with significant numbers. Almost all associations claimed to participate in HOMES, although the figures indicate that the level of activity is very low indeed.

3.19 Although mobility schemes accounted for 7 per cent of lettings in Camden, associations in the Borough reported a greater use of HOMES for moving existing tenants out of Camden (and usually out of London) compared with lettings of their own stock.

Household types

3.20 The household characteristics of those being allocated housing association tenancies in the case study areas are shown in table 3.3. This indicates that single adults under pensionable age accounted for the largest individual group of lettings in all areas except Bolton. The single elderly were the next largest group, with the elderly in general accounting for almost a third (31 per cent) of all lettings in the six area (51 per cent in Bolton).

3.21 The disproportionate number of new lettings being made by associations to single adults, the elderly and (to a lesser extent) single parent families is in part a reflection of the stock profile of associations (see table 1.5). However, it also indicates that these groups are being prioritised in allocation terms, reflecting their relative housing needs. Couples and small (two adult) families, which together accounted for over a quarter of all new applications to associations (see table 2.1) were under-represented in terms of allocations (18 per cent), in all case study areas except Bromley.

Table 3.3 **New lettings by housing associations: household type by local authority area**

	Bolton %	Bromley %	Camden %	Derby %	Exeter %	Leeds %	Total %
Single Elderly	30	22	23	14	25	24	22
Elderly Couple	21	8	2	3	12	10	9
Single Adult	17	26	30	36	40	33	31
Adult Couple	4	10	2	14	10	10	9
2 + Adults & 1/2 Children	8	17	18	11	5	4	9
2 + Adults & 3 or more Children	3	---	5	2	---	2	2
1 Adult & 1/2 Children	13	16	19	13	8	13	14
1 Adult & 3 or more Children	3	---	---	3	---	2	2
3 or more Adults	1	1	2	2	---	1	1
Base	151	121	107	343	73	368	1,163

Source : NFHA CORE Data.

Ethnic origin

3.22 The vast majority of new tenants classified their household's ethnic origin as being British/European (table 3.4). Only in Camden were there significant numbers of lettings to other ethnic groups; 19 per cent to African households and 10 per cent to both Asian and Irish households. The African households were more likely to be younger with half of the heads of household being 18-24 and a further 35 per cent 25-31.

3.23 Eighty four per cent of heads of household were white (64 per cent in Camden) and only 12 per cent black (17 per cent in Leeds and 27 per cent in Camden).

Economic activity

3.24 The CORE results confirm that new housing association tenants in the six case study areas were characterised by relatively low levels of economic activity. Only a quarter of new lettings were to households where the head of household was in full-time employment (table 3.5) compared with almost a third of all new applicants. The highest incidence of economic activity amongst new tenant households was in Bromley and Exeter (34 per cent).

3.25 Not surprisingly, the proportion of households with an economically active head of household varied considerably according to household. Childless couples, smaller two parent families and larger adult households were far more likely to have an employed head of household than other household types.

Table 3.4 **New lettings by housing associations: ethnic origin by local authority area**

	Bolton	Bromley	Camden	Derby	Exeter	Leeds	Total
	%	%	%	%	%	%	%
Asian	3	2	10	3	---	4	4
Caribbean	---	2	---	4	---	5	3
African	---	---	19	---	---	---	2
S.E.Asian	---	---	---	---	---	1	---
British/ European	95	87	53	89	99	82	84
Irish	---	2	10	1	1	---	2
Other	---	7	6	3	---	6	4
Refusals	1	1	2	1	---	1	1
Base	151	121	106	342	73	368	1,161

Source: NFHA CORE Data.

Table 3.5 **New lettings by housing associations: economic status by local authority area**

	Bolton	Bromley	Camden	Derby	Exeter	Leeds	Total
	%	%	%	%	%	%	%
Working Full-Time	15	34	20	29	34	21	25
Working Part-Time	1	5	7	3	4	5	4
Registered Unemployed	17	21	33	27	12	27	25
Retired	49	29	23	17	37	32	29
At Home/Not seeking work	11	10	8	13	4	6	9
Permanently Sick/Disabled	6	1	2	10	7	6	6
In Full-Time Education	1	---	7	2	1	4	2
Base	149	120	107	343	73	365	1,157

Source: NFHA CORE Data.

Income

3.26 CORE results also illustrates that the majority of new housing association tenants are on low incomes. Seventy per cent of households in the six case study areas had net weekly incomes of below £100 (table 3.6). In Camden the proportion was 77 per cent, although this is likely to be the case study area with the highest cost of living. In comparison, only 6 per cent of households had net weekly incomes in excess of £200, although the comparable figure was 22 per cent in Bromley.

3.27 In comparing income data for new tenants with that of new applicants (table 2.5) there is a clear indication that applicants on lower incomes are more likely to be rehoused by associations than those with relatively high incomes.

Table 3.6 **New lettings by housing associations: net weekly household income by local authority area**

	Bolton %	Bromley %	Camden %	Derby %	Exeter %	Leeds %	Total %
Up to £39.99	4	13	9	18	4	14	13
£40 - £59.99	27	22	32	20	22	28	25
£60 - £79.99	22	12	28	16	19	19	19
£80 - £99.99	15	9	8	16	13	12	13
£100 - £119.99	14	3	3	7	4	10	8
£120 - £139.99	8	5	7	6	9	8	7
£140 - £159.99	4	7	7	4	9	3	5
£160 - £179.99	2	3	1	4	6	2	3
£180 - £199.99	1	3	2	3	9	2	3
£200 or over	3	22	4	5	4	3	6
Base	141	116	101	324	68	360	1,110

Source: NFHA Core Data.

Previous tenure

3.28 In terms of previous tenure (table 3.7), 30 per cent of households in the study areas had previously been living with family or friends while more than 1 in 5 had been renting from a private landlord (2 in 5 in Exeter). As with the source (present tenure) of new applicants (table 2.4) these were the most significant tenure groupings.

Table 3.7 **New lettings by housing associations: previous tenure by local authority area**

	Bolton %	Bromley %	Camden %	Derby %	Exeter %	Leeds %	Total %
Renting - Council	23	23	32	9	16	20	18
Renting - Housing Association	3	7	7	3	8	6	5
Renting - Private Landlord	13	19	17	29	41	18	22
Owned/Buying	28	8	1	11	8	11	12
With Family/Friends	26	31	12	37	25	31	30
Other	7	12	31	11	1	13	13
Base	149	121	106	341	73	371	1,161

Source: NFHA CORE Data.

3.29 Overall 18 per cent of new association tenants had previously been council tenants (32 per cent in Camden) whilst 5 per cent had been renting from another association.

3.30 Almost 1 in 8 of new lettings during the survey period was made to households who had previously owned or were buying their own home. The figure in Bolton was a remarkable 28 per cent. Similar figures were evident in relation to the proportion of new applicants who were buying (or owned outright) their own home. The figures in Bolton are in part explained by the local authority's continued clearance programme.

3.31 The reasons for rehousing are shown in table 3.8, with households in temporary accommodation being the most significant (17 per cent) followed by overcrowding (14 per cent), health/medical reasons (14 per cent) and homeless or potentially homeless (10 per cent).

Table 3.8 **New lettings by housing associations: reason for housing by local authority area**

	Bolton	Bromley	Camden	Derby	Exeter	Leeds	Total
	%	%	%	%	%	%	%
Overcrowding	13	12	5	15	12	16	14
Under occupation	1	2	2	1	---	2	1
Poor Housing	8	3	10	12	10	7	9
Health/Medical	26	4	6	7	7	21	14
Need for Sheltered Housing	11	12	3	10	16	2	8
Nearer Family	9	7	2	3	7	4	5
Need Independence	2	4	1	9	10	5	5
Relationship Breakdown	5	6	2	5	---	5	5
In Temporary Accommodation	6	26	54	13	15	13	17
Homeless/ Potentially Homeless	9	15	6	11	10	11	10
Financial Problems	3	2	---	4	---	1	2
Harassment	1	---	4	2	---	5	3
Other		67	6	9	14	7	8
Base	151	121	107	343	73	371	1,166

Source: NFHA CORE Data.

3.32 In the two London case studies there was a greater significance attached to households being in temporary accommodation (54 per cent of new tenants in Camden and 26 per cent in Bromley) than homeless/potentially homeless (15 per cent in Bromley and 6 per cent in Camden, though many of those in temporary accommodation would have been accepted as homeless by the Council).

Summary

3.33 The pattern of housing association allocations indicates that associations are rehousing many households in serious housing need, although their ability to meet a range of needs (particularly from families) is limited by their housing stock profiles and the flow of available vacancies (see Table 1.7).

3.34 There was a good deal of consistency between associations in terms of the factors which they took into account in assessing applications. However, different associations gave different degrees of priority or weighting to each factor. A number of associations expressed the view that points and priority group systems were flawed, and that applications were best assessed on their individual merits.

Chapter 4 Nominations

Introduction

4.1 Most housing associations allocate a proportion of their lettings to applicants nominated by local authorities. This chapter describes how this system operates. Subsequently in Chapter 7 there is a discussion of strengths and weaknesses of the nomination process.

4.2 The analysis is directed at four main issues:

a) the role that nominations play in the overall context of local authority lettings and in particular how they are used to assist homeless people;

b) the effectiveness of procedures used by housing associations and local authorities to operate the nominations system;

c) the outcome of the process and how far it is fair to applicants; and

d) the relevance of the system in the context of the changing roles of housing associations and local authorities.

The role of nominations

4.3 For many years now and certainly since the early 1970's, housing associations have been encouraged to allocate a proportion of their vacancies to 'nominees' put forward by local authorities from their waiting or transfer lists. The nominations system was originally developed to organise the movement of 'overspill' to new towns, and was extended to housing associations at the time when many local authorities were assisting associations with mortgage loans and by other means. The system offered a suitable mechanism for associations to repay the help that they had received.

4.4 Since 1974 and particularly during the 1980s the Housing Corporation has taken the dominant role in funding housing associations, but the nominations link between local authorities and associations has remained. The proportion of nominations is not fixed but it is generally taken to be 50% of 'true' voids (see Glossary), though it can be more when, for example, the local authority has provided land for a scheme.

4.5 Nominations have provided a useful extra source of lettings for local authorities and have enabled them to help some groups, such as single people and those needing sheltered housing, that they might otherwise have been unable to assist.

4.6 This then is the theory. In practice, however, this study has found indications that local authorities have not given their fullest attention to nominations, at least until recently, possibly because such nominations represented a fairly small proportion of their total lettings. This position is now changing (Table 4.1). The number of nominations went up between 1989-90 and 1990-91 in each case study area where complete records were available. This increase was particularly noticeable in Bromley and Exeter. The proportion of nominations also increased in Bolton, Bromley, and Exeter but the proportion in Camden was distorted by the substantial use of private sector leasing which helped to boost the total lettings figure in 1990-91. These increases were probably due to a combination of two factors. First, there was greater concern to fully utilise nominations because of the pressures arising from homelessness and other needs and second because, in terms of new supply, housing associations are providing many more new dwellings - a trend which is likely to continue for the foreseeable future.

Table 4.1 **Nominations compared with total local authority lettings (excluding transfers and mutual exchanges) - case study areas, 1989-90 and 1990-91**

	Total lettings (including HA nominations)		Nominations		Nominations as % of total lettings	
	89-90	90-91	89-90	90-91	89-90	90-91
Bolton	2100	1788	172	215	8	12
Bromley	929	989	115	171	12	17
Camden	916	2388	143	179	16	7
Derby	n/a	1543	n/a	331	n/a	21
Exeter	282	411	14	53	5	13
Leeds	6601	6817	n/a	n/a	21	20

Note The large increase in total lettings in Camden is mainly due to the increased use of private sector leasing.
N/A = not available.
Source: Information supplied by local authorities from HIP1 returns (1990-91 figures provisional).

4.7 Looked at from the housing association's point of view nominations represent a major source of new applicants, in theory, for more than a half of their new lettings. It is to be expected, therefore, that nominations will figure more highly in their consciousness than perhaps for the local authorities.

4.8 At face value the concept of nominations is relatively straightforward, but in practice this is not so as was illustrated in the report 'Partners in Meeting Housing Need' (ALA et al, 1989). It might be expected that local authorities would have the right to nominate whoever they chose and for the association to rehouse that person, but this is not so. Often the associations ask for several names to be put forward for a particular vacancy and expect to make the choice themselves. Also there is no universally recognised means for determining which particular 'true void' is to be nominated as being available.

4.9 It was very evident from the interviews carried out for this survey that reports such as Partners in Meeting Housing Need (ibid), The Housing Corporation's Circular 48/89 (Housing Corporation, 1989) and NFHA, AMA, ADC Joint Guidance on Nomination Arrangements (NFHA et al, 1989) have stimulated reviews of policies and procedures. It is now widely understood by both housing associations and local authorities that a fundamental switch of roles is under way. It is no longer just a question of housing associations being complementary but different to local authorities - they are now seen as major providers catering for all types of need. This position will strengthen in future years.

The proportion of nominations given

4.10 The Housing Corporation recommendation is that nominations should be at least 50 per cent of true voids. This target was widely used in all the case study areas apart from Camden. In Camden an agreement was reached in 1990 to work to a higher target of 75 per cent in the case of two and three bed dwellings and to 100 per cent on special schemes funded by the Borough. A similar arrangement was also being discussed in Bromley but had not been agreed at the time of the survey.

4.11 Higher targets were frequently adopted where the local authority had contributed to a scheme by supplying land and in these cases a 75-80 per cent nomination right was usual or even a 100 per cent right in a few cases. By contrast, there were examples where associations had built schemes without public subsidy and did not feel obliged to allow nominations on these developments. Several associations gave a higher figure on their own initiative, and some indicated that they would be prepared to give more if the local authority pressed for them.

4.12 Although nominations formed a significant and growing proportion of total lettings (Table 4.1), monitoring was far from rigorous except in Camden. An impression was gained from the interviews that housing departments tended to be well aware of new build schemes and had few problems in securing the appropriate nominations, but that as far as relets were concerned there was little idea of the number that should be coming forward and little was done to check whether the appropriate proportion of nominations was being attained. There is also some support for this view from the analysis of CORE data which is examined in more detail later in this Chapter.

4.13 Nominations are compared with all lettings (excluding internal transfers) in Table 4.2. This suggests that, despite the reviews and general tightening up of systems described above, it was only in London that the 50 per cent target was achieved. This probably reflects the severe housing pressures experienced in London and hence the need to give more priority to nominations. The number of new lettings recorded by CORE over the period of the study was too small to allow statistically significant comparisons to be made between associations over the proportion of successful nominations made but it is likely that there were marked differences between them.

4.14 The shortfall of nominations which resulted from not meeting the 50 per cent target was not large in relation to total lettings by the local authority. In Bolton 50 per cent of association lettings (excluding transfers) would have led to 75 lettings and compared with an actual figure of 58 (between Oct 1990-Mar 1991) so the loss to the Council was 17 over the six month period. In Derby the loss was 46 lettings, in Exeter 12 (but probably mainly due to The Exeter Housing Society - see note to Table 4.2), and in Leeds 53. The losses would, of course, have been significant for households who were in temporary accommodation or put into such accommodation because a vacancy was not available when needed.

4.15 As explained above, the information obtained does not allow analysis of the performance of individual associations. However a number of explanations can be put forward for associations not achieving the targets set. At its simplest it could be that associations were not making the appropriate number of nominations but the matter is likely to be more complex than that. It could have been poor management. For example, some of the problems that associations reported with the pool system of nomination (described below) suggest that little thought had been given to organising an effective nominations procedure. It could also have been that local authorities were reasonably satisfied with the outcome achieved and that under-performance was not regarded as sufficiently important to make a call on scarce resources.

***Table 4.2*: Nominations compared with total housing association lettings to new tenants - case study areas, October 1990 - March 1991**

	All lettings	Nominations	Nominations as % of all lettings
Bolton	148	58	39
Bromley	120	67	56
Camden	106	77	73
Derby	342	125	37
Exeter	73	25	34
Leeds	363	131	36
Total	1,152	483	42

Notes: The proportion of nominations for Exeter is likely to be low because The Exeter Housing Society owns a large number of dwellings not subsidised from public funds and does not make nominations from these.

Source: NFHA CORE Returns.

4.16 Another explanation could be lack of demand arising, for example, because of a mismatch between the local authorities' needs and the opportunities offered by the associations. The use made by local authorities of nominations is considered in more detail below but it may be significant that some associations in Leeds, Bolton, and Derby had formed the view that the local authority did have some difficulty finding nominations for some types of accommodation in some areas (sheltered housing was frequently mentioned in this connection). All the local authorities claimed that they did not have any problem finding nominees.

4.17 It is also worth noting that the performance of the case study areas was very much in line with the general picture as shown by the NFHA CORE figures (NFHA 1991). This shows that in the last quarter of 1990 in London about 54 per cent of lettings to new tenants were to nominees while in the rest of England the proportion was 39 per cent.

The local authorities' use of the nomination system

Property type

4.18 The use that local authorities can make of nominations depends very much on the size and type of vacancies offered, which in turn depends upon the type of stock available. This is heavily weighted towards small dwellings, flats and sheltered accommodation.

4.19 In the following paragraphs the NFHA CORE returns made during the six months from October 1990 to March 1991 are examined to show who benefitted from the nominations system. It should be stressed that the sample sizes were small, especially in Exeter, and the results must be treated with some caution.

Table 4.3 **No. of bedrooms in property allocated to successful nominees - case study areas, October 1990 - March 1991**

	Bolton %	Bromley %	Camden %	Derby %	Exeter %	Leeds %	Total %
1 Bed/Bedsit	73	54	49	45	62	64	57
2 Bed	22	41	39	28	14	25	29
3 Bed	5	4	12	27	24	11	14
Base No.	59	68	77	126	29	133	492

Source: NFHA CORE Returns.

4.20 Table 4.3 shows that a very high proportion of nominations in all areas was made up of one bedroom/bedsit units. This was especially so in Bolton, Exeter and Leeds while in Bromley and Camden two bedroom units were noticeably higher. Generally the proportions of 3 bed accommodation were low though this reached about a quarter in Derby and Exeter.

4.21 Nominees however, generally received a lower proportion of one-bed properties compared with lettings made from other sources. This was true of all the case study areas except Bolton. The proportion of lettings to nominees compared with those from other sources who obtained two-bed properties was higher in all the case study areas apart from Bolton and Exeter - the difference was particularly marked in Bromley where 41 per cent of lettings to nominees were of 2 bed units compared with 33 per cent of letting from other sources and Camden (39 per cent compared with 17 per cent).

4.22 For three bed properties the picture was more mixed. The proportion of nominees allocated three bed dwellings was higher in Camden, Derby and Exeter and lower in the other areas. The figures for lettings made from other sources include internal transfers within the association and it interesting to note that in all the case study areas combined, almost twice as many three bed roomed dwellings were let to applicants from other sources (likely to be transfers) than to nominees (136 compared with 71).

Table 4.4 **Letting type of successful nominees - case study areas, October 1990 - March 1991**

	Bolton %	Bromley %	Camden %	Derby %	Exeter %	Leeds %	Total %
New Let	46	31	36	48	41	17	35
Relet	54	69	64	52	59	83	65
Base No.	59	68	76	126	29	132	490

Source: NFHA CORE Returns.

4.23 Table 4.4 shows the proportions of new lettings (new build and rehabilitated units) compared with relets of existing accommodation. This shows that the proportion of new lets was almost a half in Bolton and Derby and was particularly low in Leeds and to a lesser extent in Bromley.

4.24 It is very striking that in every case study area a higher proportion of lettings to nominees were to new lets compared with lettings from other sources. This suggests that nominations may work best when a new development is first let although it could also indicate that new developments now coming 'on stream' may be more appropriate to the needs of the local authorities. It also suggests that local authority nominees are likely to get the best quality accommodation.

Table 4.5 **Property type allocated to successful nominees - case study areas, October 1990 - March 1991**

	Bolton %	Bromley %	Camden %	Derby %	Exeter %	Leeds %	Total %
Flat etc	71	77	78	48	69	73	67
Bed-sit	3	10	20	5	0	5	8
House	25	13	3	48	31	22	25
Base No.	59	68	77	126	29	133	492

Source: NFHA CORE Returns.

4.25 In Table 4.5 the proportions of each property type allocated to successful nominees are shown. This shows that allocations to bed sitters (regarded as one of the least desirable types) were highest in Camden and Bromley and that flats and maisonettes represented a very high proportion in Bolton, Bromley, Camden and Exeter.

4.26 However, it is also the case that a much higher proportion of lettings made to applicants from other sources were bed-sits even in Camden and Bromley. As far as flats are concerned, a lower proportion of lettings to applicants drawn from other sources were made in Bolton, Bromley, and Leeds and a higher proportion in Camden, Derby and Exeter.

4.27 Table 4.6 illustrates some wide variations between areas in terms of the type of household. In Bromley, Camden and Derby families with children were the most frequent (45, 51 and 47 per cent respectively). Older people (singles and couples) were the most important groups in Bolton (63 per cent), Exeter (40 per cent) and Leeds (42 per cent). As could be expected from the type of stock owned by associations, single adults formed significant proportions in all areas and were particularly important in Derby.

Household type

Table 4.6 **Household type of successful nominees - case study areas, October 1990 - March 1991**

	Bolton %	Bromley %	Camden %	Derby %	Exeter %	Leeds %	Total %
Elderly (singles & couples)	63	22	28	6	40	42	30
Singles	14	21	18	31	20	20	22
Adults (2 or more)	2	12	4	16	12	8	9
Families with children	21	45	51	47	28	30	39
Base No.	59	67	77	125	25	132	485

Source: NFHA CORE returns.

4.28 When lettings to applicants from other sources are compared with nominations it is evident in each area, apart from Bolton, that families with children formed a much lower proportion of lettings. This difference is very pronounced in Camden and Bromley where there were hardly any direct lettings to families. On the other hand, direct lettings to elderly couples and single people combined represent a very high proportion of all direct lettings (viz 61 per cent in Bolton, 87 per cent in Bromley, 90 per cent in Camden, 63 per cent in Derby, 90 per cent in Exeter, and 72 per cent in Leeds). This suggests that associations tend to use nominations for family sized accommodation but use other sources to find tenants for their traditional client groups of single people and older people. It may also indicate that housing associations were responding to the needs of local authorities in a much more flexible way than the formal '50 per cent' system recommended by the Housing Corporation would suggest.

4.29 The high proportion of nominations going to families with children in the two London boroughs probably reflects the new approach to nominations referred to earlier in this chapter.

Transfers

4.30 The CORE returns suggest that local authorities made extensive use of nominations to transfer their existing tenants. In Bolton 42 per cent of successful nominees were recorded as previously renting from a local authority, and the equivalent figures for the other areas were; Bromley 34 per cent, Camden 91 per cent, Derby 33 per cent, Exeter 92 per cent and Leeds 51 per cent. Unfortunately, as households housed in temporary accommodation prior to nomination are also recorded as council tenants (which particularly affects Camden and Bromley), these figures cannot be taken as 'transfers' in the normal sense of the word. A small number of former local authority tenants would also have come from other areas under mobility arrangements.

4.31 Most associations reported that existing local authority tenants were only considered if nominated by the local authority. In Bolton, Derby and Leeds, however, a surprisingly high proportion of direct lettings were made to applicants who were previously local authority tenants (26, 57 and 36 per cent respectively). In Derby this proportion was higher than that for nominees with a previous tenure of local authority (33 per cent). The main reason for this appears to be that associations were prepared to consider existing council tenants for sheltered housing on a direct basis.

Homeless people

4.32 The proportion of successful nominees who were homeless is shown in Table 4.7. The table indicates a wide variation between areas over the contribution made towards the relief of homelessness. In Bromley and Camden well over 50 per cent of successful nominations were allocated to statutorily homeless people, but the proportion was less in the other areas ranging from 29 per cent in Leeds to 17 per cent in Bolton. Apart from Exeter, associations also made a useful contribution towards rehousing non-statutorily homeless people (likely to be mainly single people). This figure was particularly high in Derby where almost one third of lettings were to this group. Overall homeless people figured least often among nominees in Exeter and Bolton.

Table 4.7 **Successful nominees by whether homeless or not - case study areas, October 1990 - March 1991**

	Bolton %	Bromley %	Camden %	Derby %	Exeter %	Leeds %	Total %
Not homeless	75	29	26	48	79	59	50
Statutory-homeless	17	57	62	21	21	29	34
Non-statutory-homeless	8	13	12	38	0	12	16
Base (100%)	59	68	77	126	29	133	492

Source: NFHA CORE Return.

Reason for rehousing

4.33 In Bolton just over a half of successful nominees were rehoused for health reasons or because of a need for sheltered housing. This figure was also high in Exeter and Leeds (36 per cent and 32 per cent respectively). In Camden and Bromley, rehousing from temporary accommodation was the most important reason (55 per cent and 31 per cent respectively). Overcrowding was given as the reason in about 10 per cent of cases in Bolton, Bromley and Leeds and was highest in Derby (17 per cent). Surprisingly there were very few nominees recorded as having been moved to reduce under-occupation which is often thought to be something that local authorities try to do using nominations. It may be, however, that rehousing for health reasons or the need for sheltered housing also has the additional effect of reducing under-occupation.

4.34 It has already been commented on that in some case study areas quite high proportions of direct lettings were to those who previously had been renting from a local authority. An examination of the reasons for the rehousing of all households recorded as previously renting from a local authority (i.e. nominees and all other sources) shows even more markedly the importance of health related lettings. In Bolton the figure was 71 per cent, and for the others it was Bromley (25 per cent) Camden (3 per cent) Derby (56 per cent), Exeter (33 per cent) and Leeds (71 per cent). In Derby virtually all the health related lettings to previous local authority tenants were to direct applicants which supports the point that the associations were prepared to accept existing local authority tenants for sheltered housing on a direct basis. The very low proportion in Camden is largely explained by the large numbers rehoused from temporary accommodation who are counted as previous local authority tenants.

Nominations procedures

Which properties were nominated?

4.35 The first stage in the process was for the housing association to decide which of its vacancies should be nominated. The Housing Corporation's advice to associations is that they should offer a representative cross section of all lettings by area, quality and size and clearly from the local authority's viewpoint this could have an important effect on who they are able to nominate. The survey indicated, however, that most associations used an ad hoc approach rather than taking the decision in a systematic way.

4.36 The aim of offering a reasonable cross section of vacancies can be achieved most easily by using a systematic method, though such systems restrict the flexibility of allocations officers especially when vacancies are few and far between and very difficult choices are faced between people in serious housing need.

4.37 Where ad hoc systems are used monitoring has to be very close (and the interviews revealed that this was not the case) if a reasonable cross section of voids is to be offered.

4.38 Examples of systematic methods used are described in Partners in Meeting Housing Need (ALA et al 1989) and these include;

a) counting vacancies as true voids if the tenant had died or moved out of the housing association sector and nominating every other one of these and,

b) tagging properties from the beginning as 'belonging' to the local authority and nominating every time one of these became vacant.

4.39 It was fairly clear from the interviews with housing associations (apart from those in Camden) that the question of defining 'true' voids was not considered to be a major issue and it is doubtful whether many staff had a clear idea of what was involved. The use of a computer in allocations would, of course, make it much easier to implement a systematic approach.

The housing association request for a nomination

4.40 Where the direct system of nomination (i.e. a request for nominations for a particular vacancy) was in operation, it was usual for the association to phone or fax the local authority housing department with details of the property which had become vacant. Where the phone was used it was normally followed up with written details. Associations usually liked to receive more than one name - three was a figure frequently mentioned.

4.41 In Camden the use of the fax was considered important so that there was a record of the request, but in all the other areas respondents felt able to dealt with the staff in the housing department by phone without this causing any problems. Relationships were generally considered to be good on a day to day working basis.

Methods of providing nominations

4.42 In the case study areas it was very evident that the method the local authorities were using to nominate was changing. Two systems were in general use, the pool system and the direct nomination system. Where the pool system was in use, the trend was to switch to the direct system. There were variations over the way the pool system was operated but in outline the local authority provided the association with a list of nominees from their own waiting or transfer lists in advance of any vacancy coming up and such nominees were put on to the association's waiting list and rehoused when vacancies came up. With the direct system the association contacted the authority only at the point when a vacancy came up and asked for three or four names to be put forward for that specific vacancy. The systems used by the case study authorities are shown in Table 4.8.

Table 4.8 **Methods employed by local authorities to organise nominations.**

Bolton	Pool system with a housing adviser responsible for liaison. This was changing and larger associations were expected to request a nomination when a vacancy came up - mainly to help widen options for dealing with homelessness.
Bromley	Direct system through central lettings section.
Camden	Direct system through central lettings section.
Derby	Pool system but not regarded as very satisfactory and new systems were being considered.
Exeter	Direct system had recently been introduced because of problems with pool system - liaison through lettings section.
Leeds	Pool system organised through 38 local housing offices. Variable performance between areas and dissatisfaction with results and fast track direct system for some nominations centralised through housing advice section has been introduced (three nominations made of a similar type).

Source: Interviews with the local authorities.

4.43 The interviews with associations revealed that many problems have been experienced with the pool system. The information supplied by the authority quickly became out of date and a lot of time was wasted by associations because they were given the wrong address, found the household had changed its composition, or had already been rehoused elsewhere. A further problem was that applicants nominated could be out of the local authority's own allocation system for a long time and as a consequence could miss out on alternative rehousing opportunities.

4.44 Another problem which associations experienced with the pool system was local authorities nominating too many names and leaving it to the association to sort out what they would do with them. Several associations in one area said that the local authority had provided a list of over 100 names in response to a request for nominations. This may have been a mistake by an inexperienced member of staff but it may also indicate the lack of seriousness with which nominations were treated by that authority.

4.45 The problems of the pool system were widely recognised. In all the case study areas a switch to a direct system had either been carried out or was in the process of being introduced. Where the pool system had been extensively used in the past it was evident that it will take some time to work through the applicants who had already been nominated and put on to the association's waiting list before a switch to the direct system can be introduced.

Nominating applicants

4.46 Local authorities have to decide which of their applicants they should nominate. In the case study areas this was usually done on the basis of the local authority's own priority system but normally subject to the agreement of the applicant - a very important qualification because the tenancy conditions were different from those applying to their own tenants.

4.47 Two factors were frequently mentioned as deterring applicants from agreeing to nomination;

a) the fact that rents were often much higher for housing association lets compared with those of the local authority and,

b) the loss of the right to buy if the association was charitable (and most in the study were).

Because of these factors, local authority officers in most of the case study areas held the view that an association letting was not considered as attractive a proposition as formerly and some applicants would no longer consider one. In Exeter, for example, it was stated that tenants applying for a transfer frequently would not agree to be considered for a nomination. This is in marked contrast to a few years ago when it was frequently said that nominations were highly sought after and reserved for tenants of "good standing".

4.48 All the local authorities, apart from Camden and Exeter, asked applicants to state on the application form whether they would be interested in a housing association nomination. However, little information on what this involved was provided unless specifically requested. This lack of advice is quite worrying in the light of the general lack of awareness of what housing associations are and how they operate as revealed by the group interviews with applicants (see chapter 6). In Camden a preference form was circulated to all applicants who were close to rehousing (including homeless people) and this included a question on willingness to be nominated.

4.49 In all the areas studied, local authorities said they used the same priority system as the one operated for their own dwellings. The main proviso was that (apart from homeless people in Bromley and Derby) applicants could choose not to be considered for nomination. In Bromley homeless people were given no choice; rehousing from temporary accommodation was carried out in date order and if an applicant was due for rehousing at the time an association void was on offer then he or she was obliged to consider it. Bromley operated a one offer policy to homeless people so in these cases the applicant had little choice but to accept.

4.50 Local authorities rarely contacted applicants at the point of nomination to check whether the personal details they held such as address and family composition were still correct (though Camden were planning to do this): it was usually left to the housing association to deal with such details. This left some associations complaining about the poor information supplied by the authority and the abortive work it entailed. It would make sense for the authority to check its records as a matter of course to ensure that the details were correct. Such checks need not be extensive especially if recent contact had been made with the applicant.

4.51 In spite of the drawbacks of a housing association tenancy, local authorities said that they had little difficulty in finding applicants who were willing to be nominated, though sometimes these applicants were not those with the highest priority. The associations in Bromley, Camden and Exeter confirmed this view, but in Bolton, Derby and Leeds some associations reported that the local authority sometimes found it difficult to produce a nomination especially for sheltered housing, for bed-sitters, and for some unpopular areas.

4.52 In Bolton some associations said that it was possible to arrange with the local authority to nominate a direct applicant they wished to rehouse. This seems an unnecessarily cumbersome procedure to adopt. If the local authority cannot provide a nomination then the association should feel free to fill the void by other means.

4.53 In a number of authorities agreements had been reached over the time that should be taken for the local authority to respond to a request for a nomination. The most ambitious of these was in Exeter where the target set was 24 hours; if the City had not responded within that time, the association was able to fill the vacancy from other sources. In Camden the target was two days and in Leeds 10 days (although it was not clear why it needed to be so long).

4.54 It did not appear that targets had been established for the time taken for associations to process the nomination though this is a matter of some importance for the applicant, and suitable targets have been suggested (e.g. ALA et al 1989).

How associations allocate nominations

4.55 Virtually all associations required applicants to complete one of their own application forms. The nominee was then visited and assessed. If more than one nomination had been made the most usual approach was for the association to visit each one and then decide between them on the basis of their interpretation of housing need. In Camden, however, where nominations were prioritised, the associations (with one exception) visited the first nominee and only proceeded with the others if the first could not be contacted or refused. This saved time and did not raise expectations that could not be fulfilled.

4.56 When associations were asked how the choice was made, it was said to be on the basis of need in accordance with the association's own criteria. It was not clear how this was done when nominations were of very different types (e.g. a transfer because of harassment, a transfer to reduce under-occupation, or a homeless family) - a dilemma which can be expected quite often if the local authority is strictly following its own priority system. In Derby the local authority anticipated this problem by nominating three applicants of a similar kind, but such an approach does represent a real constraint on the freedom of the local authority to use nominations in accordance with its own priorities and in the most appropriate way. There was no equal opportunities monitoring of the characteristics of nominees who were unsuccessful.

4.57 Where the pool system was in operation the associations added nominees to the waiting list and judged them much as they would a direct applicant, even to the extent of giving them points in some cases. This illustrates another aspect of the confusion about the status of nominees compared with direct applicants which has been commented upon earlier in this chapter.

Rejection of a nomination

4.58 Associations usually reserved the right to refuse a nomination but said that this was rarely exercised. The reason most frequently given was that the household was of a size that did not 'fit' the dwelling available, or that someone in the household was not able to cope with stairs or some other feature of the dwelling was unsuitable. In a very small number of interviews it was mentioned that the associations did not have the support available to enable them to house the mentally ill. It was also said that sometimes the local authority nominated mentally ill people without informing the association of this fact.

Refusal by applicants

4.59 Associations reported that refusals were rare although most did not have figures readily available to back this up. If refusals were rare this could have been because local authorities were doing a good job "screening out" unlikely applicants before nomination or it may have been because most applicants were in desperate housing need and had little real choice in the matter.

4.60 The effect of a refusal varied between authorities. In Bolton, Derby and Leeds there were no formal restrictions on the number of offers made and each case was treated on its merits. Applicants who were homeless were often not treated as generously as other categories. In Bromley, Camden and Exeter a housing association offer was counted against the appropriate number of offers allowed. This meant in Bromley, for example, that a homeless family would receive one offer only.

Time taken to let a void

4.61 Most respondents in associations in Exeter and Bromley felt that there was little difference between the time taken to fill a void using nominations and other methods. This may be because those authorities were using the direct method of nomination and also associations considered that these two local authorities were running an efficient system. In Bromley many associations ruefully mentioned that the picture was not as good in some of the other local authority areas they operated in. In Camden associations felt that quite long delays were incurred using nominations.

Monitoring

4.62 Apart from Camden, monitoring by local authorities was not very extensive. Most had a quarterly return of numbers rehoused from the associations, but took little follow up action to ensure adherence to nominations quotas or to check on the quality of accommodation offered. A most obvious equal opportunities check that should be made is to compare the characteristics of those rehoused as opposed to those sent back when more than one name is put forward in response to a request for a nomination.

4.63 Allocations, including equal opportunities aspects, are covered when the Housing Corporation carry out monitoring visits. But these are relatively infrequent and cannot be regarded as a substitute for local authorities and housing associations carrying out their own regular checks.

4.64 Housing associations were asked if they monitored the characteristics of nominees in any way to ensure that local authorities were being fair over who they nominated. None did so, though a few expressed the view that they felt that more homeless people and more people from ethnic minorities could have been included. Clearly if these misgivings exist they should be investigated and if necessary acted upon by the associations.

Summary

4.65 Local authorities have exercised the right to nominate applicants to housing associations for many years. In the case study areas, nominations to housing associations were growing in numbers and local authorities were taking a much more serious interest in them although their own lettings were still numerically much higher. The Housing Corporation's recommended target is that 50 per cent of true voids should be nominated. This was only achieved in London (the figure was 73 per cent in Camden). The target was not reached elsewhere (it was less than 40 per cent in each case). The reasons for this were not completely clear.

4.66 A high proportion of housing association lettings to nominees were of one bedroomed properties although this proportion was even higher for direct lettings. Nominees secured a higher proportion of two bedroomed properties than new tenants coming from other sources and it seems that associations looked to offer more two bedroomed properties to the local authorities.

4.67 There were some marked differences between the areas in terms of the household type of successful nominees. Elderly people made up just under a third of lettings but comprised almost two thirds in Bolton. About a fifth of nominees were single people (almost a third in Derby). On average about two fifths were families with children and this was over a half in Camden. Over a third of all nominees were statutorily homeless, but this figure masked wide variations between London and elsewhere.

4.68 The interviews suggested that housing associations employ ad hoc methods to select which vacancies to offer to the local authority rather than a systematic system. This could lead to a failure to achieve the target for nominations or possibly, to a reduction in the average quality of property offered within the framework of any local agreement.

4.69 The local authorities interviewed employed two main methods of organising nominations, the pool system and direct nominations to particular vacancies. Many problems were reported with the pool system and in most areas the direct system was being introduced. Local authorities normally use their own allocations priority system to choose who to nominate, subject in most cases to the applicant being willing to accept nomination. In Bromley families accepted as homeless were not given a choice. It was reported in most areas that housing association lettings were no longer considered attractive opportunities because of higher rents and the lack of a right to buy.

4.70 Most associations requested several names to be nominated for each vacancy so they could chose who to make the offer to. The choice was made on the basis of the association's definition of housing need. This is a cumbersome procedure which imposes an additional and different priority system on the local authority's and can quite easily lead to unfairness. In Camden this problem had been overcome by three names being put forward in priority order and associations only contacted the second or third nominees if the first was not successful. This system does not raise false hopes for unsuccessful applicants.

4.71 Statistical monitoring of nominations by local authorities was not very extensive (apart from in Camden) and there was little follow up action to ensure adherence to nominations quotas or to check the type and quality of properties made available.

Chapter 5 Working together

Introduction

5.1 The changing pattern of new social housing provision and the increasing significance of housing associations in the overall pattern of lettings make the issue of effective coordination between local authorities and associations ever more important. This chapter of the report considers two aspects of the current working relationships between local authorities and housing associations and then examines the prospects for closer collaboration over the allocation of housing. First it assesses the process of planning local housing strategies and the roles played by associations, the Housing Corporation and the local authority. Second it looks at liaison arrangements in place between authorities and associations for making best use of the existing housing stock. Finally, looking to the future we examine the case for more administrative co-ordination in the form of common waiting lists or local registers of housing need.

Strategic planning

5.2 The study examined the planning of local housing strategies and the involvement of housing associations and the Housing Corporation in that process.

5.3 It was evident from the six case studies that although there were established routes for consultation between the 3 parties (authority, associations and the Corporation), there were no substantial mechanisms in place for developing 'joint' housing strategies between associations and authorities. This is not surprising given the relatively small number of lettings presently produced by associations but viewed in the light of the new development this becomes an issue of concern. Typically the local authorities sent copies of their HIP statement to each association (and/or circulated the statement at the regular liaison meeting; see paragraph 5.11). It was not very clear if this was intended to inform the associations in terms of their own bids to the Housing Corporation or whether it was largely for information.

5.4 Most associations were firmly of the view that they would welcome more guidance from the local authorities about housing needs though many also felt they had a contribution to make in the process of needs assessment. It was felt that this was the local authority's responsibility and that the authority was much better placed to do this. Associations were often operating in more than one authority and many had limited skills in the area of needs assessment. Only the larger associations had a real in-house research capacity. Moreover, many of their developments have been in response to directly expressed needs rather than a product of an overall needs assessment of each area. This is consistent with their role as supplementing the provision through the authority but it will become increasingly questionable as their role as providers grows.

5.5 In terms of the patterns of allocations and lettings locally, the London Borough of Camden had the most sophisticated system for monitoring and comprehensively reviewing association lettings based on its own returns from associations. This clearly gave the authority important insights into the local role of associations and a much better base for developing local strategy. No authority appeared to provide details of the aims, objectives and outcomes of their own lettings to associations except in terms of the information produced in the annual HIP return. Again it was generally felt that better information on all lettings in the social housing sector within the local authority area would be a valuable aid in informing and guiding all the agencies concerned.

5.6 The regional offices of the Housing Corporation discussed local needs with the authorities although it was clear that the local authorities were seen as the lead body in the process. The Corporation received the views of the authorities and then used this information to evaluate bids from associations and to assist its own allocation process. There was some confusion about roles. Associations relied on the local authority, recognising the theoretical role of the district council in housing needs assessment but really took greatest notice of the Housing Corporation - which was really their only course of action to secure future funding. The Corporation sought information from the authority and the associations to have a clear view of need. The authorities often felt that the Corporation should have a view as should local associations. It was evident that the Corporation had the most real power in the process because it distributed the funds. However there was some agreement that a strengthening of all the different parties' roles would be valuable.

5.7 The regional offices of the Corporation had varied levels of contact with authorities. In some cases the Corporation sat in on HIP meetings but often it was simply included in the post-HIP seminar when the actual allocation could be reviewed. It is not clear whether having the Corporation involved earlier influenced the bid made and allocation received although it could assist the process of producing a more rounded and realistic strategy. It was apparent the Corporation would welcome more contact with authorities and more information and vice versa. To illustrate this in one case study area, the Regional Policy statement for 1990/91 produced by the Corporation (London and Home Counties South) indicated that the Regional Office had written to each authority asking for written statements on local housing priorities but only half the authorities replied and in the stress areas this fell to one third of authorities. While there may have been other channels of communication this does suggest a lack of commitment to the process on the part of local authorities.

5.8 There was much greater clarity when it came to allocations as a whole and with respect to direct lettings, although not in relation to local authority nominations, associations saw the Corporation as being the key body with respect to monitoring the processes involved and the outcomes generated.

5.9 In some senses there is a duplication of roles at the local level between the authority and the Corporation. Both influence local associations albeit in different ways. However, as authorities develop their local strategies and monitor the outcomes more closely, they will move ever closer to the role played by the Corporation and this will necessitate a review of local arrangements. Moreover it is apparent that the Corporation has no local needs data beyond that produced by the authorities (and via the GNI). This may mean that local needs are poorly assessed in specific authorities.

Local liaison arrangements

5.10 In addition to meetings between the local authority and individual associations, in every case study area there was some form of local liaison arrangement. However, as Table 5.1 shows, these varied considerably. Meetings were conducted at both the political/member level and at officer level.

5.11 In general terms, these meetings were seen to be of considerable use although some were rather large and formal. The most effective work was often done in the associated sub groups when it was possible for a small group to work in detail on an issue, for example, on an information leaflet or the details of the nomination process. It was felt that there was a real need to discuss broad strategy in the main meeting but there was a feeling that this was not achieved and that much of the discussion was dominated by development issues.

Table 5.1 **Local authority and housing association liaison arrangements**

	LA Chaired Liaison meet	HA Chaired Liaison meet	Frequency of meeting	Sub Groups
Bolton	No	Yes	Quarterly	Yes (Mgmt; Devt)
Bromley	No	No [1]	N/A	Yes
Camden	Yes	No	Quarterly	Yes (Mgmt)
Derby	No	Yes	Quarterly	No
Exeter	Yes	No	Quarterly	Yes (Officers)
Leeds	No	Yes	Quarterly	Yes (Mgmt; Devt)

[1] There is no formal regular liaison but the authority is often invited to the Bromley Federation of Housing Association (BFHA) meetings and the Secretary of the BFHA is a co-opted member of Bromley's housing committee.

Source: Case study reports (unpublished).

5.12 It was clear from all of the case study areas that there was room for improvement in terms of liaison between the different parties (the authority,the Corporation and associations). There was considerable uncertainty as to roles regarding assessing need and to the adequacy of the exercise. It should be recognised that although authorities are typically much larger and better resourced than associations, there are now a number of associations with considerable resources which operate in areas where their capacity to assess need is probably no less and possibly much better than the local authority.

Common housing need registers and other new forms of collaboration

5.13 Given the developing relationship between authorities and associations, the likelihood that associations will become ever more important in terms of local housing provision and the concern to provide choice and to make allocation processes intelligible to prospective tenants, the study examined a number of possible developments in the formal relationship between local authorities and associations.

5.14 In particular interviewees were asked to comment on the merits or otherwise of developing common housing need registers (common waiting lists) and other forms of collaboration. A number of suggestions along these lines have been made but the basic concept is that all applicants for social housing should be able to complete a single form in order to join a register of those in housing need from which all organisations would be able to select households to whom to make offers. The list would be maintained by a single organisation, such as the local authority or a key local housing association, which would provide an agency service on behalf of all participating bodies. This concept could be operated in different ways; for example each organisation could continue to use their own selection criteria or a degree of standardisation over allocations policies could be introduced if so desired.

5.15 Local housing need registers (often referred to as common waiting lists) have been advanced as a means of preventing duplicate registrations on the waiting lists held by the different housing organisations operating in any local authority area and as a more convenient 'one stop shopping' approach to registering one's housing need. At present an applicant has to register separately with all the organisations in the area and this may entail a large number of visits, phone calls and letters. Local housing need registers could also provide a means of defining and dealing with needs on a more consistent basis between organisations, perhaps even leading to common allocation policies and common points schemes - although this may be somewhat controversial.

5.16 Common allocations policies are more radical in that all the organisations involved would agree a common set of policies and practices for the allocation of housing. This could include the adoption of a common points scheme.

5.17 The response to all of these ideas was varied. There was a real concern that any attempt to introduce commonality would reduce the capacity of the providers to respond to the diversity of need. This was felt to be particularly true of common allocations and points schemes. There was a general acceptance that common waiting lists were a good idea and these could reduce overlaps, save administrative time and benefit the applicants. It raised the possibility of shared home visits prior to acceptance onto the waiting list.

5.18 However it was evident that associations were worried about the loss of their own independence and it was felt neither they nor tenants might have much confidence in a common system (even if only a common waiting list system) if the local authority operated it. There was also a real concern about the practicality of any such arrangements given that associations operated across local authority boundaries although common forms could be considered as one mechanism for tackling this.

5.19 As might be expected local authorities were more supportive of the idea though they were concerned about the cost implications of any such arrangement (and a cost per applicant ratio). There was a concern that it could place the burden of cost upon the authority. Set in the context of the possibility for compulsory competitive tendering of housing management functions, a common waiting list and indeed a common allocations system, takes on a rather different perspective. It would be possible to envisage a body separate from all of the agencies concerned tendering to operate such a service and this may make the idea more acceptable to the associations who expressed concern abut a loss of autonomy.

5.20 Common local housing registers are being explored in a number of local authority areas and this included at least one of the case study authorities (Derby) although it should be noted it had been considered and rejected in Exeter. As a first step the discussion is focusing on a common application form and it is evident much could be achieved by simple steps such as this. Developments in this area will take place where there is trust and confidence and this will build up over time through joint ventures such as common application forms, common advertising and other joint arrangements.

5.21 The issue of common registers of applicants with housing needs is one of great current interest. The potential benefits for both applicants and housing organisations are substantial and progress along these lines is highly desirable. The interviews revealed interest in the concept and recognition of its merits, but also highlighted that there is some mutual mistrust and misunderstanding between the associations and local authorities. It is important, therefore, that efforts to set up joint schemes should be based upon an equal partnership between organisations. In particular, the eligibility criteria for entry to the common register must be as wide as possible and not exclude any groups traditionally catered for by any individual agency.

5.22 While there was real concern about the implications of common allocations and points schemes there was recognition that, through the nominations process, steps had already been taken down this path. Associations accepted applicants from the local authority list in accordance with agreed priorities. In London, closed waiting lists and nominations in excess of 50% were such a significant part of the housing associations' allocation process that the associations were, in essence, operating a system which was taking them towards a common list and allocations system with the authority concerned. As the case studies show London was exceptional in the importance of nominations in the associations' allocations. It does suggest, however, that as the balance of the housing stock changes between associations and authorities and as housing needs continue to rise, nominations will become ever more important everywhere. If that happens then, de facto, common systems will be in place. While all associations valued their independence there was a recognition that the movement was in this direction.

5.23 The collaboration in these areas and in the development of new property was important and bound to draw the two types of organisations together. This process would be enhanced by local authority transfers. Bromley was exploring a transfer of its stock and, if it went through, this would give further momentum to the process.

Summary

5.24 This chapter has considered the degree of integration and coordination between authorities and associations with respect to allocations and local housing strategies.

5.25 There were evident gaps in the mechanisms in place to achieve strategic planning to meet housing needs at a local level. It is important that attention is given to the issue of planning and coordination at such a level. Local liaison meetings were common although their effectiveness was questioned. Again further attention to this issue is needed.

5.26 In terms of new forms of collaboration, it was evident associations and authorities had begun to think about issues such as common waiting lists but there was little impetus behind these ideas in most case study areas. Concerns with loss of independence, the costs of implementation and the likely effectiveness of the outcome had discouraged associations and authorities from seriously evaluating ways of building new working structures. However, there was a recognition that change was likely to come in this area.

Chapter 6 Informing the consumer

Introduction

6.1 Social rented housing is, or at least ought to be, allocated according to housing need and not according to a household's ability to pay. It is therefore crucial that those in need know how and where to apply for assistance and that local authorities and housing associations as providers of rented homes communicate effectively about their policies, procedures and practices.

6.2 Those in need of social rented housing require information about the range of organisations who may be able to assist them. Applicants need information about allocation policies and practices to advise them of their chances of being rehoused, to inform them of any choices they might have which will help them in getting rehoused more quickly or in an area of their own preference, to reassure them that their prospective landlord is accountable, and to enable them to judge whether or not they have been treated fairly within the published rules.

6.3 The study has already examined the characteristics of households who have been seeking access to social rented housing in the case study areas, and their reasons for doing so, as well as the type of households who are being rehoused by housing associations. However, in seeking to evaluate the efficiency, effectiveness and equity of housing allocation policies it is also important to examine the ways in which landlords in the social rented sector provide information to potential tenants in relation to allocation policies and the experiences of the consumer in applying for social rented housing.

6.4 In discussions with housing associations the study has sought to explore how they make the services they offer widely known in the areas in which they operate. In addition, from information provided about recent applicants for social rented housing, British Market Research Bureau's Qualitative Workshop were commissioned to undertake group interviews in four of the case study areas (Bolton, Derby, Exeter and Leeds). However, because there were so few direct applicants to associations in either Bromley and Camden they were unable to conduct group interviews in these two areas. In Camden, in-depth interviews were conducted with recent housing association tenants. In Bromley in depth interviews have been held with recent applicants for rehousing to the Borough Council. Full details of this element of the study are set out in appendix A detailing the research methodology.

6.5 The group discussions and in-depth interviews were designed to enable applicants/tenants to give their perception of local authorities and/or housing associations as providers of rented housing, their reasons for applying to the local authority/housing association, their views of their experiences as applicants and suggestions they had of the ways in which applying for social rented housing could be made simpler or more responsive to the consumer.

6.6 This chapter examines the ways in which local authorities and associations provide information to applicants (and potential applicants), the views of the consumer of the access process, and seeks to offer guidance on good practice in providing information about allocation policies and procedures.

The legal and administrative frame work

6.7 In translating the objective of meeting housing need into policies and practices both local authorities and housing associations need to operate within the existing legal framework.

6.8 The Housing Act 1985 (Section 22) requires local authorities to "give reasonable preference" to:-

- People occupying insanitary or overcrowded houses.
- People living in unsatisfactory housing.
- Large families.
- People found to be homeless and to whom the Authority has a duty under sections 65 or 68 of the Act.

6.9 Sections 58-78 of the Housing Act 1985 define the duties of local authorities towards those accepted as homeless. In particular, a local authority has to:-

- Secure accommodation for those they accept as homeless or threatened with homelessness if:
  - they are in "priority need"
  - they are "unintentionally" homeless
  - they can show a local connection with the authority to which they apply.
- Provide temporary accommodation for homeless people in priority need regardless of the circumstances leading to their homelessness or their local connection.
- Provide advice and appropriate assistance to those not in priority need.

6.10 The Housing Act 1985 also requires local authorities and housing associations (except fully mutual housing co-operatives) to make available rules about the way in which individual decisions regarding tenant selection and allocations are made. The reason for this is to ensure that landlords in the social rented sector are accountable for the ways in which publicly subsidised housing is used. At the same time, it enables individual applicants to know how the selection process works and therefore judge whether or not they have been treated fairly.

6.11 Under section 106 of the Housing Act 1985 both local authorities and housing associations are required to:-

- Publish a summary of the rules by which priorities are determined between different applications (both new and those seeking a transfer)
- Have a set of rules determining the procedures for allocating housing.
- Provide any member of the public with a copy of the summary of its rules free of charge and/or a copy of its procedures at a reasonable cost.
- Permit all applicants to inspect the personal information which they have provided and which is held in support of their application.

6.12 Housing associations are also required to provide a set of their rules to the Housing Corporation and to local authorities in those areas where they manage rented housing.

6.13 The 1985 Housing Associations Act (section 15) prohibits registered housing associations from granting any benefit (and a tenancy is taken to be a benefit) to any officer, member, or employee of the association (or any of their close relatives) irrespective of their needs. Again, this does not apply to fully mutual co-operatives, where tenants must all be members.

6.14 Housing associations registered under charitable rules may also be constitutionally restricted as to the type of household they may assist. Associations operating on such rules may need to take account of tenants' incomes. The Inland Revenue may only regard an association as charitable if the majority of its tenants have below average incomes.

6.15 The Race Relations Act 1976 makes it unlawful to discriminate (directly or indirectly, intentionally or unintentionally) on the basis of colour, race, nationality, ethnic or national origins. Section 21 of this legislation specifically prohibits such discrimination in the letting of property, the terms of lettings, and in the treatment of people relative to others with similar needs. The 1975 Sex Discrimination Act makes it illegal to discriminate against anyone on the grounds of their sex by targeting her/him less favourably than anyone else.

6.16 The Data Protection Act 1984 gives individuals a right to access any computer record concerning her/himself. Information can only be legally withheld from people if it may cause serious harm to them or to a third party who supplied the information. The Tenants' Guarantee requires associations to give access to applicants to inspect their records and to correct any inaccuracies; a comparable requirement to that imposed on local authorities by the Access to Personal Files (Housing) Regulations, 1989.

6.17 Whilst the legal requirements and duties placed upon local authorities with respect to housing are extensive, for housing associations the statutory obligations are considerably less. The constraints on associations are largely non-statutory, although their continued funding may depend upon the extent to which they comply with standards set by the Housing Corporation. Guidelines have been set by Corporation circular and the requirements of the Tenants' Guarantee and Performance Expectations. These make it clear that associations have a duty to publicise their housing provision and are expected to collaborate with local housing and health authorities and voluntary and community organisations in order to make themselves known and invite appropriate applications and/or referrals. Associations are expected to use whichever means of access to their housing will identify prospective tenants in most serious need.

6.18 The Tenants' Guarantee also says that associations are expected to have clear, understandable policies and procedures for selection and allocation and ensure that subsidised housing is offered to those most in need.

6.19 There is a growing expectation in most public services that consumers are entitled to good quality information which fairly and accurately describes what is being offered. Applicants for social rented housing have to make important and far reaching decisions which are likely to affect their future quality of life significantly. It is of crucial importance that they do not miss out on housing opportunities because they have not been properly informed about what they are, how they work or how to apply. If those in the most need do miss out -and others in less need benefit at their expense - then this not only disadvantages those in need but also leads to the misallocation of scarce publicly subsidised resources. The allocation process is less efficient and effective than it might otherwise be.

6.20 So what are the views of applicants for social rented housing with regard to the services which local authorities and housing associations are providing in terms of access to housing? What are their perceptions of the process of applying for a council or housing association home, and how do they think this process could be beneficially improved?

Information needs and options

6.21 Local authorities, more so than housing associations, have an advantage in so far as they are widely recognised as providers of rented housing. Of those interviewed as part of group discussions, the great majority of those applying for housing association accommodation had heard of housing association first from friends or relatives. It is incumbent upon both local authorities and housing associations to ensure that information about the types and location of the housing which they manage, and how to apply for this, are widely available to all potential applicants. It would be helpful, however, if more information were available about the work of associations to prevent misconceptions ("the difference between the council and housing associations is that the housing associations are out for making money") and puzzlement.

> *"The housing associations stay so quiet. They're like underground cities, nobody knows they're there until the last minute. We only heard about them from a friend".*

6.22 For most applicants, local authorities are not a major source of information about housing associations; this is despite the best efforts being made in several of our case study areas to produce directories of housing associations and their properties. Leeds and Derby, for example, publish directories of associations/stock whilst Exeter have a one page leaflet listing local associations with some details of their properties and are working with associations to expand this. However, whilst communicating such information must be an essential part of providing an efficient and effective service it can be a costly and time consuming process. Documents have to be attractive and up to date.

6.23 The fact that the majority of group discussion participants had heard of housing associations from friends or relatives accords with views expressed by many associations in our case study interviews. Where associations do take direct applications and have open waiting lists, most expressed the view that applicants got to know of them by word of mouth or because they were long established and had a local presence within a particular area of the local authority district.

6.24 Respondents who were actively helped to apply to housing associations tended to be the most vulnerable, the persistent and those difficult to place, who were often referred to housing associations by agencies such as the Citizen's Advice Bureau. Local authorities were not seen as a major source of information - except in terms of ticking a box (i.e. wiling to be nominated to a housing association) or being handed a list of associations and their properties, often without comment or categorisation of the associations, leaving the applicant to contact individual associations directly. As one respondent commented "I went to the council and they didn't seem to give two tosses about it. He gave me a list of the housing associations and said I was probably better off with them than with the council".

6.25 Most respondents perceived their options as being limited to the local authority and one or two "known" housing associations. However, this may be because their "search" for rehousing is limited to particular local areas where some individual associations have been zoned to operate rather than others. A minority of group discussion participants initially only knew of the local authority and learned about associations only later in the process. However, it is possible that some respondents may have ignored guidance from the local authority about applying direct to associations due to a lack of confidence in the local council or previous experience of rejection by housing associations.

6.26 About one fifth of those interviewed did not apply to their local council at all, because they perceived it as too slow or because it offered very little prospect of rehousing or that the sort of property which the local council might offer was considered too "down market". Those not applying to the local council were particularly concentrated amongst the elderly, who tended to be concerned with obtaining good quality housing, and young single people, who expected to be offered accommodation more quickly by housing associations.

The reasons for applying to housing associations

6.27 The main reasons respondents gave for applying to a housing association were:

- The increased prospect of being rehoused or the hope of being rehoused more quickly (this was particularly so for young single people and family households).
- A desire for better quality accommodation.
- To obtain a particular type of accommodation.
- To avoid recurrent maintenance problems (particularly the elderly).
- To be near to friends/relatives or in order to remain in the same area in which they were already living (once again, especially the elderly)
- Because a trusted source had advised it.
- Because they were seen as providing higher status housing then the local council. However, although there was an almost universal preference for housing association accommodation over other options, most respondents indicated that they would accept a council tenancy if the property were suitable.

6.28 Specific housing associations were likely to be selected on the basis of local factors (area of operation, type of housing etc.) and knowing others who were already tenants or who had applied, rather than on the basis of the image of the association itself.

6.29 All groups saw housing associations as smaller than the local council (undeniably true at the local level), faster in dealing with issues/problems, and with better quality (newer, better maintained) accommodation and fewer troublesome tenants. All these factors combined to make housing association accommodation higher status than council housing.

"I'd recommend housing associations to anyone, rather than the council. But there again, if you look at the properties they've got they don't look after so many, so they can be looked after a bit better".

6.30 Some groups saw the associations as private and/or profit making. The elderly and those in Derby were particularly prone to take this view. In Leeds, and amongst a minority in other areas, associations were more likely to be seen as similar to the council, but offering better value for money and a more efficient service. Overall, there was a tendency for group discussion participants to envisage housing associations as half way between the local council and the private sector - but without the drawbacks of either. Respondents had very little understanding of who ran associations.

A consumer perspective on the allocation process

6.31 Many of the group discussion respondents had found the process of applying to their local council for rehousing either distressing or futile. A number of reasons were given:-

- Queues.
- Lack of privacy in council offices.
- Rude or uncaring attitudes amongst staff.
- Made to feel unimportant or a nuisance.
- Lack of assistance in completing application forms.
- Long delays in communication.
- Misleading/contradictory information.
- Inflexible attitudes and/or policies.

Many respondents did not find the atmosphere in council offices was conducive to asking for help, or, probably, giving it. As one respondent commented:-

"I went in and told them my situation and they just said oh, there's more people before you, like, go away - well, they didn't say that but - it was come back when you're homeless, sort of thing".

6.32 On average, respondents' experiences in applying for rehousing to housing associations was more positive. As smaller organisations they were seen as friendlier (with more polite and caring staff) and offering better access and (in some cases) more privacy for discussing housing needs. They were also perceived as likely to respond more quickly and better at keeping in touch.

6.33 However, a number of criticisms also emerged with some failing to respond to applications and some requiring information which was considered too personal (a view particular to elderly respondents in relation to requests for financial information). In general, there was little understanding of allocation procedures/priorities (as opposed to the process of applying) and some suspicions of unfairness.

6.34 Very few group discussion participants knew how their application for rehousing was being assessed. Where points systems were in use (a minority of cases), respondents had no idea of their own level of points, how their level of points might relate to others on the waiting list, or indeed how points were awarded.

6.35 Only amongst the elderly in Bolton and some young singles (in Leeds and Derby) was there a match between respondents' own situation and what they perceived housing association priorities to be. In other cases, respondents knew that associations housed people like themselves but so far had been disappointed or been given pessimistic forecasts of when the association might be able to offer them suitable accommodation. Coupled with ignorance of the allocation policy and procedures, this led to mistrust and some perception that others who can "work the system" or are "more desirable" tenants are being given priority. However, even the mistrustful saw associations as offering them an extra option - and one which gave them a better chance than the local authority, which was seen as overwhelmed by the demand for rehousing and giving priority to family households.

6.36 Respondents also had negative views of the home visit/interview process, where many felt they were being "checked-up" on and "judged". Some lines of questioning were considered intrusive whilst others saw this interview either as falsely raising expectations of being rehoused or dashing hopes. Overall, the interviewer was seen as being in control of the process with the applicant as subordinate, which discourages applicants from asking questions.

6.37 Participants in group discussions suggested a number of improvements which might be made to either the application or allocation process. These included:-

- A more active "selling" of associations at council offices.
- A check on awareness of housing associations amongst applicants.
- The production of association/property lists according to categories of housing provided.
- The use of ethnic media to publicise the work of associations.
- Minimum use of personal financial questions.
- More frequent contact and updating of position on waiting list.
- Better explanation of what an individual's level of points means (where point systems are used to prioritise applicants).
- An explanation of the way in which the nomination system works.
- More information about likely rent levels.

6.38 Although the idea of a Common Waiting List, from which all local housing associations and the council could draw, was discussed only one group (the elderly in Derby) favoured such a scheme. In other instances the local authority were not trusted to handle applications efficiently. As one applicant commented about the nomination process:

> *"When you're filling your form in they ask if you want them to nominate you for a housing association - you have to tick the box".*

"And did you?"

"No - I went and done it all myself. They (the council) take too long.

They just shove your papers to one side, leave you, they're not bothered about you, you're nowt special".

Summary

6.39 A range of legal and administrative obligations are placed upon both local authorities and housing associations with regard to access to waiting lists and allocation of available properties. However, it is clear from discussions with consumers that there remain a number of areas where applicants are uncertain of their position and the options open to them.

6.40 In practice, individual housing agencies should ensure that accurate, up-to-date, clearly written statements of allocation policy and practice are available to the general public.

6.41 The means of entry to a waiting list or housing register should be well publicised and easy to use for all potential applicants. A high proportion of applicants interviewed had discovered housing associations almost by accident rather than because of any systematic dissemination of information about them. The possibility exists that something akin to a housing association sub-culture may be developing, with application dependent on "inside knowledge". If wider application is to be encouraged, then there is a need for more positive promotion of associations to a wider spectrum of potential applicants. This might involve relevant information on associations being supplied to doctors, health visitors, local councillors and other authority figures from whom potential applicants may seek advice.

6.42 The nature and effectiveness of publicity in respect of housing associations in general may be of particular concern, since many of those in severe housing need may be unaware of their activities. Local authorities and referral agencies will need to have up-to-date information about housing associations' stock of accommodation and their particular priorities. At the same time, associations themselves need to consider how they can improve the dissemination of information about their operations to as wide a range of qualified applicants as is possible.

6.43 In those areas where there are significant numbers of ethnic minority households, care should be taken to ensure that material is reaching these groups. This may involve the provision of published leaflets and application forms in translation, as well as advice and assistance on completing forms.

6.44 As far as possible, the rules of the allocation system should be designed or worded to be easily comprehensible. It must be recognised, however, that there may be a conflict between simplicity of design and explanation and meeting a complex set of objectives. A straightforward date order waiting list may be simple to describe and understand but may have serious disadvantages as the basis for helping those in the greatest housing need as a matter of priority.

6.45 However sophisticated the allocation system, it is important that information provided to applicants is easily understood. It is best presented in a simple, attractive and readable way with the minimum of jargon and gobbledygook. More information should be made available about the different priorities and specialities of local associations.

6.46 The nomination system needs to be clearly explained (preferably verbally) to applicants so that opportunities are not missed either through ignorance or inadvertence.

6.47 It is also important that potential applicants are not deterred or obstructed by the type or complexity of information required as part of the application process. In addition, forms for applying should be well designed and produced.

6.48 Where applicants are required to give specific information or produce documentary proof (e.g. of income) then the purpose for which this information is required should be clearly explained.

6.49 Finally, in recognising that the demand for social rented housing is likely to be greater than supply in most localities, both housing associations and local authorities should advise applicants about the housing options available to them. Where applicants are accepted on to a waiting list these options may provide alternative avenues for rehousing. Where they are not accepted, advising applicants on alternatives will widen their choice.

6.50 Overall, the two basic needs are for more information and particular sensitivity in the handling of applicants who, in many cases, are likely to be suffering from stress in other areas of their lives at the time of applying for rehousing.

Chapter 7 Conclusions and recommendations

Conclusions

7.1 This study has been concerned with four main issues:

a) the current access and allocation policies and procedures of housing associations in six case study areas;

b) the process of nominations by local authorities to associations and the ways associations and local authorities work together in this area;

c) the adequacies of these systems in the light of the associations' own objectives, local housing needs and national policies on subsidised rented housing; and

d) the ways in which potential tenants come to the notice of associations.

7.2 In each of the preceding chapters a series of issues have been raised in relation to these core objectives. The purpose of this chapter is to draw together the main themes of the study, provide an overall evaluation and set out recommendations.

7.3 It is useful to begin by reflecting on the criteria which might be used to assess the relative effectiveness of the processes and outcomes of allocations and nominations. There would seem to be several possible ways of doing this.

7.4 The first is to examine the position in relation to the objectives set by the organisations concerned. Housing associations and the local authorities seek to house those with the greatest demonstrated need. The purpose of points and other allocation systems is to allow housing organisations to distinguish between applicants in terms of need.

7.5 The Housing Corporation's own performance expectation states that "Housing associations are expected to provide accommodation for those who are inadequately housed or homeless, and whose needs cannot be met at prices within their means or at all, elsewhere in the local market".

7.6 Alternatively it is equally valid to use the criteria of economy, efficiency and effectiveness as promoted by the Audit Commission (to which might be added equity).

7.7 The approach adopted here is to use all of these different criteria. Outcomes are compared to the objectives set and efficiency, effectiveness (albeit limited, because the study did not collect financial data, thus preventing an analysis of cost effectiveness) and equity are considered and assessed.

7.8 The assessment begins by drawing together the main conclusions on the issues of access to and allocation of housing by housing associations. It then moves on to discuss nominations and the working relationships between associations and authorities. Having taken stock of these key concerns, this final chapter then re-examines specific evidence provided by the survey of tenants. This leads to the penultimate section where the outcomes of the process and the findings from the analysis of CORE data (the continuous record of association lettings) related to the 6 case study areas are reconsidered. Finally all the material is drawn together in a concluding section which looks at the strengths and weaknesses of the current system and puts forward suggestions for change.

Housing association allocations: access and allocations

7.9 Interviews with associations in the six case study areas indicated that associations were providing for a diverse range of both general family and special needs housing.

7.10 While acknowledging the considerable demand for housing association dwellings, the research indicated that associations could often do more to explain the role they played in meeting local housing need, the details of their properties, and their policies and practices in relation to who may apply for rehousing and how they allocate. Small associations, with limited stock and relatively few lettings, might consider linking up with other associations and/or the local authority to ensure that the local community are aware of their services. There is, of course, little incentive for associations to advertise more widely if they are already overwhelmed by demand. Only 3 of the case study authorities produced leaflets about associations in their areas and the detail was quite limited. A lack of systematic information discriminates against those in ignorance of the available services and in favour of those with informal contacts.

7.11 Outside of the two London case study authorities, most of the associations studied had open waiting lists and allocated a substantial proportion of their available dwellings to let to direct applicants. However, from time-to-time some associations closed their lists to restrict additional demand. It is recognised that it may not always be economic, efficient or effective for smaller associations to have permanently open waiting lists. However, one solution to this may be the concept of common housing need registers (common waiting lists) considered in paragraphs 5.13 - 5.23. Others used needs based thresholds to restrict access to the association's active waiting list, though did not prevent application.

7.12 Associations varied in the restrictions they imposed on eligibility for rehousing, although generally there were few.

7.13 While access may be complicated, the study has revealed the considerable care and attention given by associations to those making an application for housing. Detailed interviews and accompanied viewing were the norm although there was evidence that this changed as associations became larger and/or under greater pressure.

7.14 In terms of those applying to the housing associations included in this study for rehousing, the research has shown that the most significant household types are single adults of non pensionable age and small single parent families. Except in Exeter, the elderly were not a significant group as new applicants. A high proportion of the applications from single adults came from those in the younger age groups.

7.15 Almost 30 per cent of the new applicants to housing associations were unemployed, with a particulary high rate amongst single adult households.

7.16 Over half of all new applicants had net weekly household incomes of under £100 per week, although almost 1 in 10 had incomes in excess of £200 per week. In a majority of cases applicants derived their income wholly from state benefits.

7.17 However, as a true measure of demand, housing association waiting lists are flawed. Almost 90 per cent of housing association new applicants were already on the local authority's waiting lists for rehousing whilst 2 in 5 were also on another association's list.

7.18 Analysis of CORE new lettings returns has confirmed that associations are meeting their primary objective of housing people in need. Allocation systems are responsive to a diverse range of needs and in many instances points systems or priority group assessments are used to set rehousing policies.

7.19 However, inherent conflicts frequently arise between the desire/need of associations to sustain their own programme of direct lettings, meet the requirements of transfer applicants, respond to requests (formal and informal) from referral agencies, and cater for local authority nominations.

7.20 The pattern of housing association allocations illustrated in chapter 3 shows that associations are reaching many households in housing need, though their ability to meet a range of needs from different household types is limited by both their actual housing stock, which tends towards the smaller housing unit, and the limited supply of available lettings. Although associations are the major providers of new social rented housing, local authorities remain the major source of rehousing opportunities.

7.21 There are real limitations on the extent to which associations, in the short term at least, can fully assist in meeting some of the most serious and pressing housing needs given the nature of their existing stock.

Nominations

How well do procedures work?

7.22 The study has shown that in most areas efforts have been made to improve the efficiency and effectiveness of nominations procedures and that where such improvements have had a chance to prove themselves they have been generally felt to be worth while. It is also encouraging that local liaison groups are discussing all aspects of nominations and allocations.

7.23 One of the least satisfactory aspects was the lack of information given to applicants about what housing associations have to offer and what nomination involves. This aspect was one that many applicants commented on in the group interviews. Local authorities need to do more to explain what nomination to a housing association means in practice.

7.24 The survey showed wide differences in the efficiency and effectiveness of procedures used by both associations and local authorities. It was evident that neither local authorities nor associations were satisfied with pool systems and the direct nomination of names in response to specific vacancies was becoming more widely used.

7.25 There was also a move towards establishing performance targets agreed by both associations and the local authority. This is a positive development but can be extended, for example, to cover the time taken by the association to complete the offer and letting. It seems reasonable that if the local authority fails to produce an applicant within a set time they should forfeit the nomination.

7.26 There is excellent good practice advice on how to improve nominations procedures (e.g. ALA et al 1989). The evidence from the survey is that when this advice is acted upon nominations can work very efficiently and effectively. There is no inherent reason why this should not be the case in any organisation if there is good management and nominations are given sufficient attention.

Multiple nominations

7.27 Many associations in the case study areas insisted that the local authority should nominate more than one applicant for any particular vacancy. This is one of the most questionable practices of the nominations process; it can raise false hopes for applicants, it can lead to lost alternative opportunities while unsuccessful applicants are out of the local authority's system, and most importantly it compromises the local authority's own assessment of priorities and is a potential source of unfairness between applicants.

7.28 Most associations argued that multiple nominees safeguarded their independence and enabled them to pick applicants with the greatest housing need. They also said that it helped them to fill voids more quickly if one of the nominees dropped out or refused an offer. These arguments are not convincing.

7.29 It was evident from the case studies that when good and well managed nominations systems are in place the time lost through refusals or for other reasons need only be minimal. In addition most associations agreed that refusals were quite rare so this should not be a significant problem. Housing associations are under considerable pressure both financially and from the Housing Corporation to fill voids as quickly as possible. If local authorities are failing to help to create good and well managed nomination arrangements then, as indicated in paragraph 7.25, it is reasonable for housing associations to look for alternative ways of minimising delays.

7.30 The point about 'independence' and the ability to choose between the relative needs of applicants illustrates the confusion that exists about the role of nominations. Housing associations are charged with providing for people in housing need; on the one hand they do this by operating their own criteria to decide between the priorities of direct applicants and on the other hand by offering nominations to local authorities (who share the general aim of providing for those with the greatest housing need). The associations however, tend to confuse these two separate means to a common end and want to add their own criteria to priority assessments already made by the local authority. In many cases the criteria for assessing applicants are different and adding an extra layer of assessment simply distorts the process. If, for example, a local authority has a strategy for creating vacancies in its own family homes by transferring existing tenants (who may be well housed) but who no longer need such large accommodation, the housing association's own criteria are irrelevant.

7.31 This confusion needs to be resolved and the precise ownership of nominations clarified. It would seem reasonable for the local authority to have complete responsibility for choosing one nominee for each vacancy in line with its own priorities; though it could have the option of nominating more than one applicant if circumstances were appropriate (e.g. if the vacancy was of a particularly unpopular type). This should however, be linked to greater efforts by the local authority to work out an effective strategy for using nominations in consultation with the associations. The effort needs to go into devising a strategy and communicating this as clearly as possible to the associations rather than into making multiple nominations.

The use made by local authorities of nominations

7.32 Much of the current debate about nominations is concerned with the direct assistance that associations can provide local authorities in relation to homelessness. But that issue can only be properly appreciated within the more general context of the use that local authorities make of nominations. It must be appreciated that local authorities work within two very important constraints - the type and size of the property available (a high proportion of flats, single person accommodation and sheltered units) and the willingness of applicants to be nominated (sometimes those with the highest priority are not prepared to be nominated). These two reasons may, in part, explain the often heard complaint from associations that local authorities nominate people in less need than their own direct applicants.

7.33 Notwithstanding the points made above, the issue of the level of housing need of nominees is clearly one which concerns housing associations and one which local authorities should address. It is not necessarily a 'bad' thing if some nominees are not themselves in the greatest housing need provided that such moves are part of a clear lettings strategy and are made within a well defined set of priorities. In addition, the reasons for such moves must be explained to the associations and accepted by them. Published allocations policies should include specific reference to nominations and describe how they are to be used - it is not realistic to simply assume they can be used in exactly the same way as internal vacancies.

Homelessness and nominations

7.34 There can be little doubt that the publicity surrounding the issue of homelessness and nominations and the increased pressures on local authorities have led to more homeless people being rehoused by associations (see for example NFHA, 1991).

7.35 There are, however, a number of general points that can be made in relation to this issue. The first is that housing associations have a much higher proportion of one-bed dwellings and flats in their stock and this is not the type of accommodation most in demand by homeless people. The position is changing and new schemes are producing more family dwellings thus increasing the potential for rehousing homeless people, but it will take time.

7.36 Second, housing associations can and do help with homelessness by indirect as well as direct means. As mentioned previously it is important that the local authority has an overall strategy for maximising the use of its own stock and considers how nominations can play an effective part in this.

7.37 Local authorities have sometimes been accused of not considering homeless people for nomination because the vacancies were considered 'attractive' lettings and therefore reserved for favoured groups such as transfer applicants (this may no longer be true as the lettings are not so highly sought after). In the study areas nominations were widely (but by no means exclusively) used for transfers, but to some extent this reflected special needs such as medical transfers and sheltered housing. It is also the case that some groups of applicants enjoy a favourable bargaining position over the choice of dwelling they are offered especially when the move is being promoted because of the council's own interest.

7.38 Housing associations have been accused of discouraging local authorities from nominating homeless people because they are regarded as being potential 'problem' tenants. This was not the expressed policy of associations in the case study areas and some indeed complained that local authorities did not nominate enough homeless people. Apart from emphasising the points made above which indicate the practical constraints on the ability of housing associations to rehouse homeless people, it is not possible to comment any further on the truth of this accusation. If such problems do arise the local authority should refuse to go along with any 'hidden agenda' of this kind and, if necessary, take the matter up with the Housing Corporation which has responsibility for monitoring and performance.

7.39 Both local authorities and associations will remain vulnerable to the kind of accusations mentioned as well as other equal opportunities aspects, unless they have very explicit allocations policies and carry out very careful monitoring (both operational and statistical) to demonstrate that their policies are fair and are being followed. The CORE monitoring system provides a very useful basis for statistical monitoring and should be more widely used.

7.40 It must be recognised that housing associations will face some difficult choices as they are required to expand their service to provide for a wider range of groups in need. There is a danger that if too much emphasis is placed on the issue of direct provision for the statutory homeless this will lead to neglect of the needs of other groups, and particularly of single people, who have had to rely very largely upon housing associations to provide them with decent housing opportunities. Neglect of this group would mean that the problem of homelessness would not be solved but would resurface in a different form.

Are local authority nominations still needed ?

7.41 The nominations system has been in operation now for over twenty years, and in that time housing problems and policies have changed considerably and are set to change even more. It is reasonable, therefore, to consider whether the nominations system needs to be substantially revised or even abandoned altogether.

7.42 Of the reasons that can be advanced for its retention, there are three that have considerable weight. The first is that many local authorities have used their own resources to provide associations with loans and subsidised land and in return have entered into nomination agreements which clearly must be honoured (although it may be possible to renegotiate the terms of such agreements).

7.43 The second reason is that some local authorities are finding it very difficult to meet their statutory obligations to rehouse homeless people, and to a lesser extent to provide for decants when modernisation programmes are undertaken. This problem, however, is largely concentrated in London and other major cities and does not apply everywhere.

7.44 The third reason is that local authorities need access to good quality stock of the right size and type in the right areas: it is not just a question of numbers. As long as local authorities have substantial portfolios of property to manage they will need to make the optimum use of them and where possible give consumers some opportunity to express choice. This involves management transfers, for example, moves to reduce under-occupation, moves to protect tenants from harassment and moves to reduce overcrowding. Organising such moves is crucially dependant upon being able to offer vacancies which are attractive to applicants and available at the time they are needed. If the local authority is cut off from such opportunities this could present them with many difficulties, unless that is, present policies which restrict their ability to provide their own new dwellings are reversed.

7.45 Many would say that local authorities also need nominations to rehouse applicants from their own waiting and transfer lists. But this is a much more debatable proposition. While most applicants continue to look to the local authority for rehousing and register with them, this proposition may have some force. If however, applicants were to become much more aware of the opportunities provided by housing associations, then it would make much more sense for them to apply directly to the associations rather than to go through an unnecessary filtering by the local authority: provided that is that associations continue to select their tenants from among those with a clear housing need and in accordance with their own published priorities and monitored by the Housing Corporation.

7.46 This, of course, raises further questions about the possibilities of local authorities running registers of housing need on behalf of all social housing agencies in their area and other steps to improve administrative co-ordination to benefit applicants; these matters are considered further later in this chapter.

Nominations agreements

7.47 The arguments outlined above suggest that there is still a case for retaining a nominations system, if not everywhere, at least in areas where pressures on the local authorities are greatest. If this is the case, there is an obvious need to tailor the arrangements much more closely to the needs of the local authorities and to the abilities of the associations to meet those needs; that is to say more co-ordination and planning.

7.48 The 50% of true voids 'norm' is arbitrary; it does not reflect varying needs between areas or of varying ability of associations to contribute to meeting these needs. The system which provides for a higher percentage of family accommodation to be nominated which has been introduced in Camden and discussed in Bromley points the way to more flexible arrangements.

7.49 A possible approach would be for the contribution of housing associations to be negotiated between local authorities and either the individual associations themselves or associations acting collectively. The agreed strategy might produce a figure much less than 50% or much more for any given area. There were indications from the case study areas that things are already moving in this direction.

7.50 There is a need for greater fluidity between all social housing but this is hampered by the central issue of unfairness - why should anyone (particularly an applicant with a chance of a council house) choose to accept an association tenancy when rents are higher and there is no right-to-buy. Not all applicants qualify for housing benefit so rent differentials do have a real deterrent effect. This unfairness, of course, also applies to direct applicants to housing associations: the fact that they have made a choice to apply to an association as well as or instead of to the council is of little comfort if their housing need is desperate - they hardly have any choice. There is a need for a more "level playing field" if applicants are not to be disadvantaged and choice widely restricted.

Recommendations

7.51 It will be evident from earlier comments that the conclusions are based both on direct evidence and assessments of what is happening. In setting out to make recommendations the report follows a similar path. In this section there are a number of recommendations which are considered worthy of further exploration and consideration. In putting these forward we are conscious that a parallel set of recommendations have been made in the two recent related reports ' Partners in Meeting Housing Need' (ALA et al, 1989) and the Royal Borough of Kensington and Chelsea's "Housing Associations Allocations Audit" (LRC, c. 1989). It is our view that both are worthy of further consideration in conjunction with the conclusions and recommendations of this report.

7.52 The recommendations from this study fall into 3 categories. First a number relate to detailed operational issues involved in the processes of allocations and nominations; second a series of more strategic concerns related to monitoring; and third a set of more speculative recommendations related to future possibilities.

Allocations and nominations

Points system

7.53 While the need for flexibility and discretion is recognised, there is a strong case for suggesting all associations should adopt points based systems of allocation. There is already a general move in this direction and away from merit related systems and it is suggested that this should be encouraged further. Points offer a more evidently objective method of allocation and can be easily published to assist potential applicants. Even small associations should be able to adopt relatively simple needs based allocation systems.

Annual lettings plans

7.54 The pressures on many organisations mean that no real overview of lettings is taken on an annual basis with this being used to guide allocations in the subsequent year. A more structured approach to allocations by preparing an annual lettings plan would encourage consideration of the priorities and provide a basis for discussion with local authorities.

Prioritised Direct System for nominations

7.55 The evidence from the study does suggest that authorities should cease operating pool based systems for nominations and should instead adopt the direct system. This means that authorities will nominate an individual household or, exceptionally, a small number of households in priority order for each specific vacancy rather than simply giving associations a pool of applicants from which the association can make its own selection. The pool system is less widely used than before, and perhaps it should no longer be used at all.

Time limits

7.56 In order to improve efficiency and service to applicants a set of time limits should operate for nominations. Authorities should respond to associations within 24 to 48 hours on receipt of property details. Associations should have two weeks at maximum from time of nomination (perhaps allowing for some allowance for the elderly) to let the property once names have been forwarded by the authority and the associations should notify the authority within 48 hours of the outcome of the offers made to the named and prioritised nominees.

Quality of the property

7.57 Ensuring a fair allocation of property to direct lettings and via nominations is difficult. The system adopted in Kensington and Chelsea of allocating every second true void to the nominations system has merit. Careful consideration should be given to this system or to other means of ensuring a systematic way of allocating property to ensure there is no unjustified bias.

Training and guidance

7.58 There is a real need to train staff to operate the nominations system. Nominations are complex and potentially time consuming. Training and the preparation of a proper manual of guidance would aid the creation of a more efficient and effective system.

Strategy

Information and awareness

7.59 Urgent attention should be given by both associations and authorities to the evident lack of knowledge which most residents have about associations. This affects the flow of applicants in a variety of ways and may well disadvantage particular groups. There are a number of issues to consider. First there is a need for a general awareness campaign on associations. The Housing Corporation and the Department could play a major role in this along with the NFHA. Second, there is a need for local advertising targeted at specific groups which both the authority and associations should participate in. For instance it is clear local authority tenants have little knowledge about associations and yet the flow of tenants from one to the other type of organisation could be important. Pamphlets, prerecorded TV monitor programmes in LA offices and local adverts could all assist. Assessments of new lettings will point towards under/over representation and help suggest where adverts might be targeted.

Local housing strategies

7.60 There should be an agreed mechanism for developing local housing strategies. This will involve annual review and planning meetings. They should be based around a needs assessment by the local authority with additional inputs by the associations, the Corporation and the Department.

Monitoring

7.61 A formal monitoring system should be adopted by all local authorities with respect to associations in their area. The system operated by LB Camden had considerable merit and was worthy of replication elsewhere. Data should be collected on refusals, the quality of property allocated and other key measures.

Customer satisfaction

7.62 A system of 'quality control' should be introduced with a random sample of all association tenants being asked to comment on their experience of the application/allocation process. This would provide invaluable feedback to associations and authorities and provide a means of assessing the effectiveness of current arrangements, at least in relation to those who become association tenants.

Statistical information

7.63 There needs to be a thorough reconsideration of the data available about associations. The Housing Corporation should ensure a full reconciliation of the data produced about the stock of individual associations and should ensure a 100% response before publishing data (or use estimates). The Corporation also needs to publish a breakdown by authority of the stock (both existing and new) of each association by bedroom size and to review data requirements of external customers.

7.64 CORE data from the NFHA must be made more accessible and it should be available to authorities. This would allow local authorities to monitor the local situation much better. There are parallels between CORE and its potential and the information now made available from the Council of Mortgage Lenders in their publication Mortgage Finance Quarterly.

The future

7.65 The recommendations here are more speculative but it is important to raise two key issues.

7.66 The future poses fundamental changes to both associations and authorities in terms of their relative roles. It is possible that nominations will become ever more vital for authorities and this will in turn raise questions about the merits of the current system of nominations. It is also possible that under the arrangements for compulsory competitive tendering such arrangements would be replaced by lettings contracts. Clearly, careful consideration has to be given to future arrangements in the light of the emerging shape of social housing provision and the role of authorities and associations and secondly with respect to changing contractual arrangements for local authority housing management.

7.67 The future could be very different from the present or the past. However it is evident that associations and authorities have sought to retain their old relationships and attitudes with respect to nominations. Thus associations put considerable emphasis on their independence and freedom of action while, at the same time, seeking and gaining a more central and thus more constrained position with respect to social housing provision. As the major providers of additional social rented housing, they will have more limited choices about who to accept as tenants. They need to play a full and clearly defined role in meeting housing need.

Common registers of housing need

7.68 In these circumstances there is a powerful case for a radical shake up of allocation mechanisms. The arguments for setting up local registers of housing need are already strong : applicants would benefit from "one stop shopping" and possibly a wider range of rehousing opportunities whilst in aggregate housing organisations could achieve cost savings. Such registers could also allow organisations to work together to adopt a more consistent approach to defining housing need. However, if such schemes are to succeed they must be both efficient and effective, thereby securing the confidence of applicants. Both housing associations and local authorities must adopt an open-minded approach to the subject. They must be established on the basis of an equal partnership between associations and the local authority.

7.69 Provocatively, it can be argued that nominations are a very inefficient process consuming considerable staff time and resources for little benefit and were conceived in very different circumstances from those that apply today. The solution to these problems may lie in moves towards a more co-ordinated approach incorporating existing nomination arrangements. Local housing need registers, or even common allocations, do not of necessity mean the loss of independence by housing associations any more than the UCCA system of university entrance compromises the rights of individual universities. It should also be remembered that independence is not open-ended. All social housing agencies are expected to provide homes for those in the greatest housing need and at the end of the day have to account for the extent to which they achieve this.

The level of nominations

7.70 Finally the study questions the rationale of the standard 50% nomination right. Some authorities need more, others less and this suggests it should be locally negotiated rather than applied as a standard. A minima may need to be specified but in some areas what is needed is 100%. Again the 50% reflects past circumstances and may sit oddly in the emerging future.

Appendix A Glossary of terms used in the report

Charitable Status	Housing associations which are either registered with the Charity Commissioners or which have charitable rules. Such associations are excluded from the right to buy provisions of the Housing Act 1980. Charitable housing associations may be charitable companies, trusts or associations.
Direct System of Nominations	Under this system nominations are made to housing associations for specific vacancies. In this case the local authority may or may not rank nominees (typically 3 or 4 households) in priority order.
Enabling Role	The actions taken by local authorities to facilitate the activities of housing associations and private developers. Enabling activities include the analysis of housing need, the development of a housing strategy, the allocation of land for housing, and partnership schemes with other development agencies. The later often include the provision by the local authority of subsidised land. The Government would like local authorities to concentrate on the enabling role rather than on the direct provision of housing services.
The Housing Corporation	A Government agency which promotes, supervises and finances housing associations. All housing associations which receive public funds must be registered by the Housing Corporation.
Performance Expectations	A guide, issued by The Housing Corporation, which sets down the standards expected to be found in an efficient and well managed housing association. It recommends that associations produce an annual report which shows how well they measure up against the expectations.
Pool System of Nominations	The pool system involves the local authority providing associations with a list of nominees from their own waiting or transfer list in advance of vacancies occuring. As associations re-house from the pool the local authority is asked to provide new nominations
Sheltered housing	Self-contained housing for elderly people where independent living is backed up by the availability of regular on-site help from a warden and alarm systems to attract help in emergencies.
Tenants' Guarantee	This was first published by the Housing Corporation at the end of 1988 to cover new assured tenants of housing associations. It reintroduced many of the 1985 Housing Act "Tenants Charter" rights for new housing association tenants.

True Void	A void that enables a housing association to rehouse a new tenant (i.e. new to the association). True voids are normally created when new dwellings are built or rehabilitated, when a tenant leaves to buy or rent from another landlord, or when a tenant dies.
Transfer Applicants	Tenants who apply to their existing landlord for a transfer to another property. Local authorities often ask their transfer applicants if they would agree to be nominated to a housing association.

Appendix B Summary of research methodology

The research was broken down into four inter-linked stages:

1. Case study interviews with the local authority, larger housing associations and the regional office of the Housing Corporation in 6 local authority district areas. The semi structured questionnaires used with associations and local authorities are reproduced as appendix C of this report.

2. Monitoring of new lettings by the participating housing associations in the case study areas over a six month period, 1st October 1990 - 31st March 1991. This information was provided to us by the National Federation of Housing Associations (NFHA) as an analysis of a sub set of their CORE returns from participating associations over the two quarters of the survey.

3. Monitoring of new applications to participating associations in the case study areas over a six month period, 1st November 1990 - 30th April 1991. The log sheet used to collect this information, which was similar to that used by the NFHA in its CORE monitoring, is reproduced as appendix D of this report.

4. Small group discussions and in-depth interviews with selected new applicants, to explore the rehousing options they had considered.

The six case study areas were selected to reflect a range of different housing situations and to give a reasonable geographical spread. However, the areas were not specifically chosen to be "representative" of all areas but to give a cross section of housing association activity.

Within each of the selected case study areas, associations with more than 100 dwellings in management (at March 1990) - 75 dwellings or more in Bromley - were invited to participate. Only two associations declined to do so. The number of associations interviewed in each area was as follows:-

Bolton	9
Bromley	12
Camden	7
Derby	6
Exeter	4
Leeds	14

Interviews were carried out between October 1990 and June 1991.

Associations interviewed at stage one of the research were asked to provide information on individual new applicants for rehousing over a six month period, 1st November 1990 - 30th April 1991. Twenty five associations across the six case study areas provided such information. The total number of applications received in relation to each authority was as follows:

Bolton 652

Derby 1083

Exeter 192

Leeds 2072

In the two London authorities, there were too few direct applications received by associations (with most lettings being made as a result of nominations or referrals) to make analysis a worthwhile exercise.

The lettings data was provided by the NFHA from CORE returns by participating associations. The total number of lettings (excluding transfers) over the period October 1990 to March 1991 by the participating associations was 1175.

In the tables produced in the main body of the report the base figure for individual tabulations of new applicants and new lettings do vary. The principal reason for this is missing individual values of particular variables. At the same time percentage figures in individual tables have been rounded up or down to the nearest whole number. As a result columns do not always add to 100%.

The final element in the study involved nine group discussions and six depth interviews.

The group interviews were with:-

Young Singles (aged 18-24)	Leeds, Derby and Exeter
Families (with children under 16)	Leeds, Bolton and Exeter
The Elderly (aged 60+)	Bolton and Derby
Couples (aged 18-35, no children)	Derby

Four in-depth interviews were held in Bromley (one elderly, one family, one couple and one young single household) and two Camden applicants were also interviewed in depth (both young singles).

Interviewing was carried out by British Market Research Bureau and included respondents' reasons for housing need; their awareness of available options, their understanding of the application process and allocation policies and their image of different providers of social rented housing.

Appendix C Questionnaires used for field work interviews

UNIVERSITY OF WALES COLLEGE OF CARDIFF

CENTRE FOR HOUSING MANAGEMENT AND DEVELOPMENT

HOUSING ASSOCIATIONS ALLOCATIONS POLICY

HOUSING ASSOCIATION INTERVIEW SCHEDULE

NAME OF ASSOCIATION:

INTERVIEWEE:

POSITION IN ORGANISATION:

DATE OF INTERVIEW:

LOCAL AUTHORITY:

SECTION A: BACKGROUND

TOTAL NO. OF SELF-CONTAINED DWELLINGS
IN MANAGEMENT (AT 31.3.1990)

TOTAL NO. OF SELF-CONTAINED DWELLINGS
IN MANAGEMENT IN CASE STUDY AUTHORITY (AT 31.3.1990)

NO. OF NEW LETTINGS MADE BY THE ASSOCIATION
IN CASE STUDY AUTHORITY (1.4.89-31.3.1990)

PROFILE OF HOUSING STOCK IN CASE STUDY
AUTHORITY (AT 31.3.1990)

	NO. OF UNITS HOUSES	FLATS
BEDSIT		
ONE BEDROOM		
TWO BEDROOM		
THREE BEDROOM		
FOUR BEDROOM		
OTHERS		

Are any of these for Special Needs?
If so, what proportion?

MENTALLY ILL/LEARNING DIFFICULTIES
ELDERLY
DISABLED
OTHERS

How many **additional** self-contained housing units do the Association anticipate taking into housing management IN THIS AUTHORITY (NAME) during 1990-91.

How many of these will be

	HOUSES	FLATS
BEDSIT		
ONE BEDROOM		
TWO BEDROOM		
THREE BEDROOM		
FOUR BEDROOM		
OTHERS		

How many of these for Special Needs?

N.B. SEEK TO OBTAIN COPY OF MOST RECENT ANNUAL REPORT

Of the lettings made in 1989-90 what proportion were made to ....

NEW DIRECT APPLICATIONS

TRANSFER APPLICATIONS

L.A. NOMINATIONS

OTHER REFERRALS

OTHERS
(PLEASE EXPLAIN)

In the case of (A) LOCAL AUTHORITY NOMINATIONS

and (B) OTHER REFERRALS

What proportion of these applicants were statutorily homeless?

SECTION B: ELIGIBILITY FOR HOUSING

Eligibility for housing

Who is eligible to apply?

How do people get to know about the services of the Association?
(OBTAIN COPY OF ANY PUBLICITY MATERIAL)

Is any publicity material translated into minority languages? If so, which ones?

Are any special measures taken to encourage applications from ethnic minority groups or any other special groups of potential applicants?

Does the Association keep a waiting list for those seeking direct access to association accommodation? How many households are currently on this list?
(IF NOT, SEEK DETAILS OF HOW APPLICANTS ARE DEALT WITH)

How is the waiting list operated?
(OBTAIN DETAILS)

Check following points are covered:

(i) open at all times or closed sometimes?

(ii) are separate lists maintained for different types of household, different size properties or different schemes?

(iii) how is each applicant assessed?

What information is given to applicants who apply, but after assessment, are not accepted on to the waiting list? (Check for time to respond and whether the association is prepared to pass on bad news honestly).

How is it decided who to rehouse? Do you operate a points scheme for those on the waiting list? If not how do you decide who should be made an offer? (OBTAIN COPY OF H.A.'s ALLOCATION POLICY)

What is the Association's policy on allocating property by size, type and area?

Do you have any hard-to-let or unpopular properties? If so, how are these allocated?

How does the Association deal with requests for transfers from its existing tenants?

How many of the Association's own tenants are currently seeking a transfer?

Do you think your allocation policy favours existing tenants or new tenants?

Do you participate in H.A. HOMES. If so, how much use is made of it?

In addition to DIRECT APPLICATIONS, NOMINATIONS from L.A. and H.A. HOMES how else does the Association receive applications for housing?

Are there any agencies from which the Association takes REFERRALS?

If so, who are these agencies?

How are referrals dealt with by the Association?

Can you briefly describe how lettings are made?

ENSURE THE FOLLOWING POINTS ARE COVERED

(i) Is viewing accompanied or unaccompanied?

(ii) Is there a restriction on the number of offers made?

(iii) What happens if a DIRECT APPLICANT refuses an offer?

Does the association monitor the following for the purposes to ensure equal opportunities.....

(i) Applicants?

(ii) The Waiting List?

(iii) Offers?

(iv) Refusals?

COLLECT BRIEF DETAILS

Are you aware of any problems over equal opportunities?

Do you have any formal system for performance review?
(BRIEFLY DESCRIBE). Do you set targets, and if so what are they?

SECTION C: LOCAL AUTHORITY NOMINATIONS

What proportion of the Association's lettings does the L.A. have a right to?

Are there any exceptions to this general rule?

Is there a written local agreement between the Association and .... District Council over nominations?

(IF SO, MAY WE OBTAIN A COPY?)

Is there an agreed definition (between the Association and the Local Authority) of what constitutes a "true void"? How is this defined (i.e. what is included and what is excluded)

Is there a specific officer within the Association who is responsible for nominations from .... District Council?

If so, who is this?
(NAME/POSITION)

Who do you liaise with in the local Authority?

How does the nomination system work?
(COLLECT DETAILS)

How does the Association inform the Local Authority about potential vacancies?

Does the Association have a standard form providing property details which is used to request a nomination from the Local Authority?

If Yes - MAY WE OBTAIN A COPY?

If No - What information is provided by the Association when requesting a nomination?

How does the Association first request a nomination from the Local Authority?

Is there a time limit for the Local Authority to put forward names? If so, how long is this?

How well do you think the system works?

Do you think a different system for Local Authority Nominations would be preferable?

If so, how would this differ from the present arrangements?

What do you see as the advantages/disadvantages of this alternative system?

Does the Association require nominees to complete a housing association application form prior to allocation?

What assistance is available to complete application forms?

Do you arrange to interview nominees prior to allocation?

If so, where do these interviews normally take place?

Are nominated households given a choice as to where an interview takes place?

When making an offer does the Association inform the Local Authority?

If so, how is this done?

On what grounds, or in what circumstances, would the Association reject a Local Authority nomination?

What happens if an offer of accommodation is refused by a nominee?

Is there a limit to the number of offers made?

What proportion of nominees do refuse an offer of Association accommodation?

On what grounds do nominees refuse accommodation?

Does the Association ever offer nominees alternative housing other than that for which they have been nominated?

If so, under what circumstances?

Do you ever rehouse a L.A. nominee in your Association's property but in another Authority area?
If so, under what circumstances?

When and how does the Association notify the Local Authority about the result of a successful nomination?

What is the average time taken by the Association to let a vacant dwelling?

On average, is there any difference in the length of time taken to let a property subject to nomination from the Local Authority compared with those allocated to households on the Association's own waiting list?

Do you do any monitoring of the nominations made by the L.A. to see that they are being reasonable over the types of applicant nominated?
(COLLECT DETAILS)

Could I just recap to make sure. What are the differences between the way you allocate to your own applicants and to nominees?

SECTION D: GENERAL LIAISON ARRANGEMENTS

Is there a liaison group (between the Local Authority, the Housing Corporation and local housing associations).

Who organises and who attends?

What is its remit?

CHECK WHETHER IT DEALS WITH POLICY/PRACTICE ISSUES AND OR INDIVIDUAL CASES

How often does it meet?
(IF POSSIBLE OBTAIN COPIES OF MINUTES)

How effective do you think these arrangements are?

What, if any, improvements could be made?

How much of a co-ordinating role do you think the L.A. play in their area...

(a) over informing you and other associations about the housing needs of the area?

(b) over allocations and lettings policy

Do you think the local authority should play more of a co-ordinating role...

(a) over assessing housing needs?

(b) over allocations and lettings policy and practice?

Could you explain the role the Housing Corporation play in informing you of the housing needs they expect you to meet?

Do the Housing Corporation have much of a say over your allocations and lettings policies.
If so, how do they monitor this?

Do you think there is any duplication between the L.A. and the Housing Corporation over their roles in assessing needs and allocations policies? (COLLECT DETAILS)

What are your views about the following suggestions:

(a) A common waiting list?

(b) A common allocations policy?

(c) A common points scheme?

SECTION E: THE FUTURE

Does the Association propose to change its Allocation policy or practices in the near future in any way?

If so, how and why?

How do you see the future for Association in working with the Local Authority and/or local Referral Agencies in meeting local housing needs through allocations?

UNIVERSITY OF WALES COLLEGE OF CARDIFF

CENTRE FOR HOUSING MANAGEMENT AND DEVELOPMENT

HOUSING ASSOCIATIONS ALLOCATIONS POLICY

LOCAL AUTHORITY INTERVIEW SCHEDULE

NAME OF LOCAL AUTHORITY:

INTERVIEWEE:

POSITION OF ORGANISATION:

DATE OF INTERVIEW:

SECTION A: BACKGROUND

TOTAL No. OF SELF-CONTAINED DWELLINGS IN LOCAL AUTHORITY STOCK (AT 1.4.1990)

No. OF NEW LETTINGS MADE BY THE AUTHORITY IN 1989-90 (1.4.1989-31.3.1990)

How many of these were to:-

A. HOMELESS HOUSEHOLDS

B. TRANSFER LIST APPLICANTS

C. THOSE ON THE LOCAL AUTHORITY'S WAITING LIST/HOUSING REGISTER

D. OTHERS (Please specify).

PROFILE OF HOUSING STOCK IN CASE STUDY AUTHORITY

	HOUSES	FLATS
BEDSIT		
ONE BEDROOM		
TWO BEDROOM		
THREE BEDROOM		
FOUR BEDROOM		
OTHERS		

No. OF L.A. DWELLINGS SPECIALLY DESIGNED OR ADAPTED AND INTENDED FOR USE BY:-

A. THE ELDERLY - SHELTERED UNITS
- OTHERS

B. THE DISABLED - WHEELCHAIR ACCESS
- OTHERS

How many additional self-contained dwellings do the Local Authority anticipate taking into housing management in 1990-91?

How many of these will be....?

	HOUSES	FLATS
BEDSIT		
ONE BEDROOM		
TWO BEDROOM		
THREE BEDROOM		
FOUR BEDROOM		
OTHERS		

How many of these will be.....

For the Elderly? - Sheltered Units
- Others

For the Disabled? - Wheelchair Access
- Others

SEEK TO OBTAIN A COPY OF AUTHORITY'S MOST RECENT HOUSING STRATEGY AND INVESTMENT PROGRAMME

How many households were on the Local Authority's Waiting List/Housing Register for council housing (as at April 1st 1990)?

Do you have a more up to date figure than this?

Do these figures include those seeking a transfer within the Authority's own stock?

How many council tenants were seeking a transfer as at April 1st 1990?

Do you have a more up to date figure than this?

OBTAIN COPY OF L.A. ALLOCATION POLICY AND APPLICATION FORM

SECTION B: NOMINATION ARRANGEMENTS

What information does the L.A. provide to waiting list/transfer list applicants about housing associations operating within the District?

When applicants apply to the L.A. for housing/ rehousing are they asked about whether that wish to be nominated to a housing association?

How many housing associations manage self contained housing within the District?

Can you tell me where these are?

How many nominations did the L.A. make to housing associations during 1989/90?

With how many associations does the L.A. have nomination agreements?

(IF POSSIBLE, OBTAIN COPIES OF ANY WRITTEN AGREEMENTS)

Is the proportion of L.A. nominations the same in each of these associations?

If no, how and why does it differ.

Is nomination to a housing association restricted to only those applicants who have indicated that they would consider taking a housing association tenancy?

Is there an agreed definition (between the L.A. and local housing associations) of what constitutes a "true void" (for nomination purposes)? How is this defined? (i.e. what is included and what is excluded)

Is there a specific officers within the Authority who is responsible for nominations to housing associations?

If so, who is this?
(NAME/POSITION)

Is there a local authority/housing association liaison group concerned with nominations?

If so, what is its name?

How often does it meet?
(IF POSSIBLE OBTAIN COPIES OF MINUTES)

Who chairs the group?

Who regularly attends?

What does it deal with? Is it primarily concerned with general policy/practice or does it (also) deal with individual cases?

What system exists for the local authority to make nominations to housing associations (i.e. How are nominations made?)

What advantages do you consider this system has?

Are there any disadvantages?

How many nominees are put forward for each vacancy?

If more than one, are the nominees in any order of priority?
How is this done?

How are nominee households selected?

Who makes this selection?

Are the "standard details" provided to associations for each nominee?

If so, what information is included?

What information is given to applicants by the L.A. when they are nominated to a housing association?

CHECK: DOES THIS INCLUDE AT THIS STAGE THE ADDRESS OF THE PROPERTY?

What proportion of nominations are of households accepted as homeless by the Local Authority?

Are nominations to housing associations considered as offers of accommodations by the authority itself?
What is the authority's offers policy?

What if a nominee refuses what is their final offer? Does the L.A. ask the housing association to keep the offer open while the case goes to appeal?

If so, for how long?

How do individual associations request nominations from the local authority?

Is there a time limit in which the Authority must put forward nominees?

How do housing associations notify the Authority about the results of nominations?

Once again, is there a time limit for doing this?

What proportion of nominees do refuse an offer of a housing association tenancy?

On what grounds do nominees refuse?

Do local Associations ever offer nominees alternative housing other than that for which they have been nominated? If so, under what circumstances?

On average, how long does it take to fill a housing association vacancy with a local authority nomination?

What arrangements are there to monitor the results of
L.A. nominations to individual associations?

What information is used as part of the monitoring process?
(CHECK - Does this include reasons for refusal)

Does the L.A. carry out an annual review/analysis
of nominations (successful rehousings/rejections)?

Are reports presented to Committee on a regular basis
on monitoring of nominations?
(IF SO, CAN WE OBTAIN RECENT COPIES)

SPECIAL SCHEMES

Are there any special needs housing association developed schemes which accept L.A. nominations?

How are plans developed to ensure a fair allocation
of special needs properties to include relevant local
authority nominees?

If so, what proportion of these schemes are allocated to L.A. nominations?

How are the nominations made?

SECTION C: THE FUTURE

Does the L.A. propose to change its own policy or practices on allocations in the near future? If so, in what ways?

How does the L.A. see the future for working with local housing associations to meet housing needs through nominations

Are there any ways in which you see local nomination arrangements/procedures are likely to change in the near future.

Appendix D New applicants log *(see over)*

STRICTLY CONFIDENTIAL

UNIVERSITY OF WALES COLLEGE OF CARDIFF
CENTRE FOR HOUSING MANAGEMENT AND DEVELOPMENT

HOUSING ASSOCIATIONS ALLOCATION POLICY
NEW APPLICATIONS LOG

University of Wales
College of Cardiff
PO Box 906
Cardiff CF1 3YN

☎ (0222) 874462
Fax (0222) 874845

NAME OF ASSOCIATION:

LOCAL AUTHORITY AREA:

NAME OF APPLICANT:

CURRENT ADDRESS:

CODE:
(Office use)

---

1. HOUSEHOLD CHARACTERISTICS

	RELATION TO 1	AGE	SEX	ECONOMIC STATE (Code)
PERSON 1	——			
PERSON 2				
PERSON 3				
PERSON 4				
PERSON 5				
PERSON 6				

2. HOUSEHOLD FORMATION

3. ETHNIC ORIGIN

4. NETT WEEKLY HOUSEHOLD INCOME (EXCLUDING HOUSING BENEFIT)

£ REFUSED/ DON'T KNOW

5. TOTAL SAVINGS OR CAPITAL

£ REFUSED/ DON'T KNOW

---

6. Is Any Household Income derived from state benefits?

WHOLLY	PARTLY	NO	DON'T KNOW

7. Does anyone in the household receive an occupational pension?

YES	NO	DON'T KNOW

8. Is the household likely to qualify for Housing Benefit when rehoused?

YES	NO	DON'T KNOW

---

9. PRESENT TENURE

10. PRESENT LOCATION- L.A. NAME

11. NUMBER OF CURRENT BEDROOMS - ENTER NUMBER

12. REASONS FOR SEEKING REHOUSING :-

13. Already on Local Authority Waiting list? YES NO

14. Already on Other Association's Waiting List? YES NO

15. Accepted on to this Association's Waiting List YES NO

NEW APPLICANTS LOG

INSTRUCTIONS FOR COMPLETION

This survey is intended to include all households who make an application to your association for rehousing in .... during the period 1st November 1990 to 30th April 1991. Please EXCLUDE those who merely enquire about accommodation without making a formal application and existing tenants who are requesting a transfer or who are being decanted between the associations properties.

The log (attached) is designed to be completed by the association and not by the individual applicants. The most reliable information is likely to be obtained from an interview but it may be obtained from the household's application or from information provided by a referral agency.

For each question please enter required information, appropriate code (see below) or circle appropriate box.

LIST OF CODES

1. ECONOMIC STATE

1. Working full-time (over 24 hours a week)
2. Working part-time (24 hours or less a week)
3. On Government Training Scheme
4. Registered Unemployed
5. Fully Retired
6. At home/not seeking paid work
7. Full-time Student
8. Permanently sick/disabled
9. Child/at school
10. Other, over 16 years old.

2. HOUSEHOLD FORMATION

1. Continuing
2. Newly Forming
3. Separating
4. Other - please describe

3. ETHNIC ORIGIN

1. Black Asian
2. Black Caribbean
3. Black African
4. White European
5. Other - please describe
6. Combination of above groups
7. Question refused

4. PRESENT TENURE

1. Renting from Local Authority
2. Renting from Housing Association
3. Renting Privately
4. Owing/Buying
5. Living with Family/Friends
6. In Bed and Breakfast
7. Hostel
8. Institution
9. Other - please describe

Associations are requested to return all completed one page logs at the end of every month, so that preliminary analysis can take place. These should be returned to:

Centre for Housing Management and Development
University of Wales College of Cardiff
P.O. Box 906
Cardiff CF1 3YN Tel: (0222) 874462

THANK YOU FOR YOUR COOPERATION

Appendix E Bibliography

Association of London Authorities et al. (1989)
Partners in Meeting Housing Need
London, National Federation of Housing Associations

Department of the Environment (1991)
Housing Association Tenants
London, HMSO

Housing Corporation (1989)
Performance Expectations
London, Housing Corporation

London Research Centre (c. 1989)
Kensington and Chelsea Housing Associations' Allocations Audit
London, LRC

National Federation of Housing Associations (1987)
Standards for Housing Management
London, NFHA

National Federation of Housing Associations et al. (1989)
Joint Guidance on Nomination Arrangements
London, NFHA

Printed in the United Kingdom for HMSO
Dd.0297758, 3/94, C4, 3396/4, 5673, 276740.